THERE'S
ANOTHER
WAY

Javier Gómez Marrero

There's another way: The path that leads to life could not have occurred to us, and that is good news for everyone.

Original title: Existe Otra Manera, originally published in Spanish in 2025 by Javier Gómez Marrero. Translation assisted by Words-AI, with full revision and proofreading by Steven Lausell.

Published by: Javier Gómez Marrero

Spanish edition proofreading: Georgina (Gina) Delucca

Cover design: Valerie Carlo Pérez

Ilustrations: Johel Gómez González

General consultant: Samuel J. Gómez González

Art Consultant: Mariel González Mercado

Legal advisor for the brand: Javier A. Gómez González

Sponsor: Kelvin J. Gómez González

Photography: Evelyn González Mercado

All rights reserved.

Reviews

"There's Another Way" integrates sound theological analysis with everyday reality, offering practical biblical responses to common human struggles, such as fear, anxiety, and the search for identity. The author addresses contemporary issues such as emotional exhaustion, information overload and spiritual disconnection, to the extent that he invites us to walk with the True Jesus. Each chapter is designed to lead the reader to personal introspection and spiritual renewal, focusing on the best news of all time.

Dr. Rafael Candelaria, President
Seminario Teológico de Puerto Rico

In a precise and clear way, my friend and Pastor Javier Gómez invites us to walk along a radically different path. It is possible to face the complexity of life and grow in the process because God specializes in redeeming suffering. A book that shepherds the soul with a challenging and practical perspective, centered on the Gospel, which manages to discern the enormous contemporary challenges. Thank you for inviting us to meet people in the real world where God is glorified when we choose to trust Him, rather than ourselves. There's definitely another way...

Dr. Nando Steidel, Pastor Cayey Catacumba Church
President - Board of Directors of Catacumba Church, P.R.

This captivating work invites us to recognize, and to transcend, the unjust social expectations that, regardless of the era, nourish the tortuous life outside of paradise, promoting and normalizing them. Dr. Javier Gómez presents us with the greatness of the Gospel of Grace, thus giving us back the blessed hope of a faith that redeems suffering. And in the meantime of the "already but not yet", he challenges us to continue trusting in the Lord in order to live a true spirituality. I hope this reading will be as much of a blessing to you as it certainly has been to me.

Rev. Iván De la Torre, Superintendent
PR District Assemblies of God USA

Learning to contemplate the sufficiency of the Gospel of Jesus for our daily lives could not be more urgent (or more relevant). Among competing paradigms, Pastor Javier Gómez Marrero exalts Jesus and His Good News as the only way to truly be what we were created to be. In these warm pages, you will find an invitation full of grace and compassion, written by someone who, by the power of the Spirit and in the merits of Jesus, has traveled something of the way and invites you to discover how to live a preview of heaven today.

Rev. Gabriela Martínez Seda, Evangelist
The Alliance – PR District

On these pages, Pastor Javier Gómez shares his heart and confronts us with the reality that surviving in this world is not the same as flourishing. At the same time, he invites us to a process of formation by opening our hearts and placing our trust in the only One with whom it is only possible to have a full life, highlighting the sufficiency of Christ and the inexhaustible treasure that is his Gospel. I consider this book to be a gift from God to all those who, like me, have felt that we are surviving, but long to flourish for the glory of God.

Rev. José Ahmed Pérez
Pastor Catedral de la Esperanza, San Juan, PR

Living to the fullest based on the opinion and identity that our God gives us is truly liberating. "There's another way" is the invitation to confront ourselves with our "false-self", and begin the process of identifying areas that need to be attended to and surrendered at the feet of Christ so that we can then resume the walk designed by God in freedom, trusting fully in Him, for who He is. Enjoy hearing the voice of the Lord through this work!

Zahydée M. Guzmán, Ed. D(c).
Director of Peacemaking Ministry
The Alliance – PR District

As a colleague and friend, I appreciate Javier's slow and truthful words. No one knowingly believes a lie, so unmasking them becomes imperative. Don't read this book in a hurry, as you might miss out on the precious opportunity to know the truth about your significant value and genuine identity in Christ. I can testify that Javier is not just writing about a theory, but rather about a freedom he has personally experienced. I firmly believe that reading this book will result in a devotional, liberating, and refreshing experience.

Rev. Timoteo Wendel
Director of Missions for Latin America, The Alliance

The best definition of prophecy is that it is a reading of the world, of the state of it, from the divine perspective. It entails both a clarity anchored in God's truth, and an understanding of the world and its present order. Dr. Gómez manages to diagnose the contemporary world with the sorrows that affect today's human being, and prescribe to them the truth of God, the Gospel. In this sense, this book represents what the church is called to be, a prophetic community that discerns the times and applies the Gospel. The Gospel is then both the correct framework for interpreting the world, for diagnosing it, and the prescription for dealing with that evil. As you approach these pages you will be able to see areas where you have been de-formed by the world and, with God's favor, begin to experience the other way of living that Christ offers us in his Gospel as we are re-formed by his Holy Spirit.

Dr. Ramón M. Meléndez Morales
Senior Pastor CD Alliance Church
Corporate Secretary of Dexcom, The Alliance – PR District

Words of Thanks

How could I ever do justice to the immense number of people who have contributed to my formation, including those who didn't even know that was precisely what they were doing? So, to all of them, thank you very much, because they all had something to do with me being able to write what I share next. A special thanks also goes to all those who encouraged me to write, my wife, my children, my family of origin and extended family, my seminary students (STDPR), and the alliance family in Puerto Rico. The C&MA La Cumbre holds a special place in my heart because in addition to being the church where I have had the privilege of serving the longest (22), it became my family. Dear church, you taught me more than I could ever teach you. I'm thankful for those who read the manuscript and improved it: Ramón Meléndez, Dinorah González, Gabriela Martínez. I'm also thankful for my friend Steven Lausell's full revision and proofreading of the English version. I thank my son Kelvin for sponsoring the editor's corrections, and my wife Evelyn González Mercado and my son Johel for helping me choose the title. And, to those who, believing that God will use this work for His Glory, wrote the prologue and the reviews. I am also grateful to my sister-in-law Mariel González (and my brother-in-law William) for allowing me to have significant retreat times once a year in their cozy home.) Especially I want to recognize my wife Evelyn for her unconditional support, as well as for her wise and loving counsel as God wrote this work in our lives and hearts, long before I put it on paper.

Dedication

I dedicate this work to my beloved parents Miguel Ángel Gómez Rodríguez and Aida Luz Marrero Serrano, whom I miss every day as they already dwell in the presence of the Lord. I also dedicate it to my brothers Miguelón and Carlos; to my wife Evelyn; to my sons Javier, Kelvin, Samuel, and Johel; and my daughters-in-law Gabriela and Valerie. But I especially want to dedicate it to my beautiful grandsons Noah and Timothy, and to those other beautiful grandsons and granddaughters who, by the Grace of God, I anticipate will be born to me in due course.

A personal invitation

In one of the films directed by Peter Jackson based on the wonderful work of J.R.R. Tolkien, the scene that moves me the most appears in the first installment of The Hobbit trilogy. In it, Gandalf, the grey wizard, invites the young Hobbit, Bilbo Baggins, to take part in what would become the adventure of his life. The two are sitting in the cozy living room of Bilbo's residence, when Gandalf tries to convince Bilbo to go, by telling him, "When you return from your own adventure, you will surely have more than one story to tell." To which Bilbo reacts by asking, "Can you assure me that I will return from this adventure?" "Not really," Gandalf replies, "and if you come back, you won't be the same person."

I want to invite you to read the following pages making Gandalf's words my own. Wishing that at the end of your own adventure you will not be the same person.

TO GOD BE THE GLORY

TABLE OF CONTENT

Prologue

When he accepted his current role, overseeing the churches of our denomination on the beautiful island of Puerto Rico, my brother, Dr. Javier Gomez had no way of knowing that in the next few years his leadership challenges would include hurricanes, earthquakes, financial crises and a global pandemic. Not only has his leadership been stretched, but his soul has been enlarged.

I was scheduled to preach in Puerto Rico the week that the COVID-19 outbreak went viral. Javier and I agreed that it was in everyone's best interest to cancel the event. Instead, a few months later, as the pandemic continued, I asked Javier to speak to our staff for an on-line chapel service. He had much wisdom to share with us arising from a gracious spirit. Most memorable to me was his statement, "Leaders who lead out of fear make poor decisions."

In authoring his first book, Dr. Gomez has been fearless in looking deeply into his own soul and aiding us in doing the same. With keen insight into both the human condition and the Holy Scriptures, the author strengthens us with hope that a better story can be written in our own lives. The spirit-crushing characteristics of a broken world—pressed in by the mold of commonly held beliefs—need not keep their grip on us. Instead, these chapters offer insights and pathways to regaining our true humanity.

The pages of this book roll out like a welcome mat, inviting us to refuse the labels pressed upon us, but to instead take the identity that the Heavenly Father desires to grant us. Accepting this invitation frees us from the oppressive burden of defining ourselves.

Years of careful reflection on the truths of God's Holy Word, combined with the wisdom that comes from living out real-world, real-life spiritual leadership have coalesced in the words you are about to read. Enter in and let your soul be enriched.

Dr. John Stumbo, 12th President
The Christian and Missionary Alliance U.S.

Introduction

Tired Souls

*"You are a soul made by God, for God... That means
that you were not made to be self-sufficient."*

— Dallas Willard
American philosopher and author
1935-2013

On Sunday, February 2 of this year, Evelyn and I
reached the significant milestone of 34 years of marriage. While
it's true that marrying the love of your life can make time seem
to fly by, three and a half decades are a lot of years. So, apart
from God, no one knows me as well as my wife and best friend.
Evelyn could easily confirm that she has been hearing me say
a phrase that could very well describe most of my life. And that
insistent phrase is: "I have to..." As in I have to fill out that
report. I have to address that problem. I have to balance that
budget. I have to attend that meeting. I have to get a pastor for
that church. I have to help that governing board. Oh, and I
have to finish writing this book!

My experience, after almost 57 laps around the sun, are
tells me that we all do that very same thing. Including the person reading this sentence (if the *I have to* bouncing around in
your head allows you to finish reading it). We all assume that

we are just one additional *I have to* away from "making it", however we may have defined that, only to immediately discover
that behind that *I have to*, there is always another one, and then
another and another and another.

The idea that our performance determines our value
and our sense of security permeates our being in such a way
that it affects every aspect of our lives. This begins to happen
as early as our cradle days. Thus, we are continually exposed to
the most severe scrutiny based on our performance, including
our own. Even our funeral will be evaluated. Fortunately, we
won't hear that last criticism.

When my first grandson was born, not three hours had
passed, when they were already informing my daughter-in-law
that little Noah had gotten a good grade in his first neonatal
exam. After finding out, we joked a bit about it, but I immediately became very serious. After a moment of silence, standing
right next to his crib, we assured Noah that we were freeing
him from the brutal pressure of having his value and sense of
security determined by his grades. And that our love would
never depend on his performance. I pray that God helps us
fulfill that promise.

You may have already noticed that justification by
good performance or good works does not belong exclusively
to the religious sphere. Incidentally, both spheres (the secular
and the religious) are irremediably intertwined. Especially as
both seek to respond to the human aim for happiness.

There are very good reasons to think that performance
justification, whether secular or religious, is not the best way to
live, let alone flourish. Measuring life based on performance

results in the most unfair and exhausting constant manipulation of our image along with the corresponding damage control efforts. Disappointment will inevitably be the norm. So, by not envisioning some other way to measure life, sooner or later we learn to resign ourselves to our performing metrics.

Twenty years ago, I had the privilege of leading a short term mission trip to the beautiful nation of Nicaragua, a country with which Puerto Rico shares the valuable story of our immortal baseball star, Roberto Clemente. On New Year's Eve 1973, Clemente suffered a fatal plane crash while on his way to Nicaragua with humanitarian aid for the survivors of a terrible earthquake. I will never forget my trip to Nicaragua, because 30 years after Clemente's accident, they continued to remember that sacrifice and thank me for it on behalf of their beloved people.

On our mission trip the group provided clothes, books, and athletic shoes to various communities that would make good use of them. One of these communities lived on a mountain that served as a garbage land fill for the surrounding city. Unimaginably, entire families lived there.

When I arrived at the place, the first person I greeted was apprehensive and doubtful. He was a man in his 30s. He asked me what I was doing there, as he walked menacingly towards me, with a piece of wood in his hands. Once my local companions informed him that we would not use him for any kind of philanthropic propaganda, and he having recognized one of our own, his attitude changed.

My now kind host offered to show me his workplace. We moved about twenty feet west, and pointing to a mountain of trash he said, "That's where I work... Do you want to meet my family?" he asked me. "It would be a pleasure," I replied. He then led me another 6 or 7 yards south, and stopping in front of another bundle of garbage let me know that we had arrived at his house. Then, when a little boy of about three years old ran towards us from a pile of empty cans, the man said to me: "I present my son to you, ah, and behind him comes my wife." At that moment, the child's mother arrived to take him in her arms. They lived among piles of garbage carefully balanced and arranged to provide a minimal degree of shelter. But what surprised me most was how they could distinguish between one pile of garbage and the other. Because one would be his house, another his neighbor's, and another his workplace.

Several beautiful things happened from that visit, because God gave us marvelous experiences there. But I mention it because I want to share with you what I said to myself that morning. "Javier, that young father is you. And so is all humanity. We live among piles of garbage, and we do not see that this is just what we do, having no other reference than piles of garbage." We fight over garbage. We long for other garbage. And we moved from one pile of garbage to another, never being able to conceive of living outside the landfill. But how could anyone conceive of such a thing, without first having sighted any glory that could serve as a reference?

WE LOST OUR WAY

Nothing could better describe what we observe in the world and in ourselves than that expression used by Jesus in describing our condition: "Lost."[1] We don't know where we come from, we don't know what we're here for, we don't know where we're going, much less who we are. But we also don't want to stop along the way to ask for directions. We're too proud for that. And yet, the desire for change expressed by many suggests that the world itself has already acknowledged that it has lost its way. Our differences are not in admitting that there is a problem, but in what we would consider to be the best remedy. A tense dynamic that will end up creating other problems for us, since everyone tries to defend their particular diagnosis, and their multiple solutions. So, if the world's problems are overwhelming, what will happen when you add the impact of unsolved local problems, including those at the household level?

Regardless of the degree of difficulty of the problem that lies before us, at the end of the day, we will try to address it in our own way. Or at least in the way which our culture considers best; according to our so-called common sense. That's why, when someone stands between my problem, and my particular solution, the result is unlikely to be the best version of myself.

ONLY ONE THING IS NECESSARY

Martha's strong rebuke to her distinguished guest Jesus would seem to confirm the above: "But Martha was distracted by the big dinner she was preparing. She came to Jesus and said, 'Lord, doesn't it seem unfair to you that my sister (Mary

---

[1]   Luke 19:10 NLT

of Bethany) just sits here while I do all the work? Tell her to come and help me'".[2] But Jesus' unexpected response would change Martha's perspective, and life, forever: "My dear Martha, you are worried and upset over all these details! There is only one thing worth being concerned about".[3]

There are so many implications here that I'm tempted to take many directions. But I will limit myself to looking at the one that, it seems to me, manages to group them together. Jesus does not seem to be saying that there is only one need. What I do think he's saying is that there's only one essential solution. A solution so significant that it will end up impacting all our needs: Having access to a life in God, with God, and for God that is supposed to define our entire existence, making it not only possible, but especially meaningful and joyful.

The good news is that, through Jesus, God has done something wonderful about that. Inviting us to return to his once inaccessible kingdom, which has now come near to us.[4] And also to discover, as Mary of Bethany did, that instead of trying to quench all our thirst and existential emptiness by ourselves — with thousands and thousands of *I have to* — now we only "have to" Jesus.

THE WAY OF JESUS

Martha's prayer, and Mary's, are therefore worlds apart. And in case you hadn't noticed, both women are praying. But obviously, praying is not enough; and neither is praying more.

---

2   Luke 10:40b NLT
3   Luke 10:41-42 NLT
4   Mathew 4:17

It is also necessary — to pray better. And the best prayer is not the one that tells Jesus what to do. The best prayer is the one that silently seeks to listen to every word that comes from Jesus. There are prayers that, thank God, Jesus will never answer, such as, for example, Martha's prayer.

Filled with anxiety, Martha tries to control Jesus. She was scared! Afraid that there was too much work for her to have to do alone. Fear always screams at us so that, at all costs, we try to have what we think we need. If that fear comes to control us, we will hardly be able to hear anything else. Martha's anxiety has reached such decibels that it translates into demands on Jesus himself. And so, her prayer ends up being about what even Jesus *has to* do.

But that's not praying. Prayer is essentially about listening to, and obeying, God. Do you want to know what the secret to God speaking to you is? Listening. But said is easier than done, as our noisy internal sense of scarcity doesn't allow us to focus. Therefore, we have not begun to pray well when our mind is already wandering off, seeking to address the infinite deficit that often characterizes our restless inner world.

I suggest that the next time you try to pray, instead of struggling with the inner noise as with an interruption, you inquire about the real reason hiding behind that noise. You might ask yourself something like, what do I think I need that, thanks to Jesus, I no longer need? In my case it's usually that I have to do something immediately or solve something that is supposedly in my charge. Noisy thoughts that prevent me from being in the present moment. Rushing, worrying, and anticipating the future. So I've learned to tell myself things like, "I'm not in charge of anything anymore, Jesus is in charge. I can be here now, because God is already taking care of everything." And so, as I apply the Gospel to my anxiety, the noise dissipates, and I get back to praying.

Justification by performance in no way appeases our fear, rather it exacerbates it. Because the yardstick with which we evaluate ourselves and each other is impossible to meet, humanly speaking. Condemning us to a cycle of shame that, as we continue to fall short, will always go from bad to worse. So we will hide from each other, and even from ourselves. Imagine then how much more we will try to hide ourselves from God as well. A real solution would be for the soul to rest from the impossible task of justifying itself, thus leaving such a heavy burden to the only one capable of carrying it. Then we would no longer feel so anxious, fearful or incapable.

We are people with tired souls. What's more, I suspect that, if we all lived long enough, then the incidence of burnout would be 100%. What sets us apart right now is not how many of us are tired, but how tired we are. Can you identify? How is your soul? Would your soul appreciate a bit of that restorative silence that can only be achieved with the cessation of our virulent fear? Allow yourself then to confide to Jesus how much hurt, guilt, shame, and decision making you have tried to handle on your own, until now. That faith placed moment by moment exclusively on Jesus, changes everything.

It was precisely because of this trust in Jesus that Mary of Bethany was able to begin to say totally different things to herself. Thus, embracing another way of living. Starting with learning to tell yourself things like: "I don't have to be in charge of everything anymore." "I don't have to do three things at once anymore; I'll do just one." "I don't have to be perfect

anymore; I can make mistakes." "I don't have to please everyone anymore, it's okay to say: No." "I don't have to know everything either, I can say: I don't know." "The judgment of another no longer defines me, Jesus does." "Only one thing is
necessary – to trust Him."

NOW I JUST "HAVE TO" JESUS

To assume for ourselves the prerogative to act in God's
place exacerbates our situation and generates anxiety. We are
not supposed to live in that way. Our hurried and overbur-
dened lifestyle does violence to our multiple limits, and therefore to our own humanity. That perennial rush can cause our
needs (perceived or real) to compete with each other for our
attention at any given moment. For it is precisely in achieving
the satisfaction of all these needs that the peace that continues
to elude us would lie. But, although it may seem too good to
be true, in the wake of Jesus' work, only one thing is really necessary. And now we just have to... I just have to... Jesus.

Now any other apparent priority can come to occupy
the secondary, tertiary, quaternary, or quinary place that corre-
sponds to it. For all that was necessary for my peace, has been
done once and for all by the only one capable of doing it—
Jesus. Therefore, now I only "have to" Jesus.

Only one thing is necessary and since I have discovered
it, no one will take it away from me. Although this world will
never cease in its determination to do so. That is why I should
not take the simplicity of the gospel for what it is not, because
learning that other way of being human is a challenge in itself.
We are facing something radically different from anything we

are used to. That is why I wish to invite you to explore more closely the only way to be human that finally aligns with the reality that is there. The only way of existing that will really make us flourish. And believe me when I tell you that your weary soul will be deeply grateful.

PART I:

THERE HAS TO BE ANOTHER WAY

Javier Gómez Marrero

Chapter 1

Our New Normal?

"… Cowards die many times before they die; the brave taste death only once."

— William Shakespeare
English playwright and poet
1564-1616

Navy SEALs are a U.S. military special forces known for intervening in some of the most hostile and unstable conditions on our planet. This military body has coined an acrostic that is very descriptive to refer to such conditions. They call them — V.U.C.A. conditions, because they are always volatile, uncertain, complex, and ambiguous situations.

Those are precisely the conditions that would seem to best describe many of the things that are happening today in most parts of the planet. Pastor Mark Sayers has referred to this moment in history as a gray zone.[5] By that he means that we live in a moment of transition between what was, and what is about to be. One era is ending but is still partially with us, while another era is beginning but not quite here. This creates dynamics and challenges that should also be classified as V.U.C.A. conditions.

---

[5]   Mark Sayers, A Non-Anxious Presence: How a Changing and Complex World will Create a Remnant of Renewed Christian Leaders. (Chicago, IL: Moody Publishers, 2022), 25.

In the case of my country, Puerto Rico, we have already lost count of the crises in recent years. The 2020 Census indicates that we were the jurisdiction in the United States that lost the most population with about 12%, which translates to almost half a million inhabitants.[6] Emigration that has continued after COVID-19. The earthquakes in the south of the island shook our soil, but also our spirits. The economic crisis continues to roar strongly. The polarization caused by our differences of opinion on issues related to the pandemic — masks or no masks, open or not open, face-to-face or non-face-to-face, and vaccine or non-vaccine — has come to stay. In addition, hurricanes are becoming more frequent and more powerful every year. Adding to the current demographic trend that has raised serious concerns is a very low birth rate, almost 60% fewer births than 30 years ago.[7]

Beyond Puerto Rico (PR), the world has been witnessing a war in Europe and another in the Gaza Strip. Not to mention the immense wave of people who have been displaced from their homes by the countless violent conflicts that continue to overwhelm the human race and characterize our times.

---

[6]   State Data Center de Puerto Rico, 2020 Census Results for Puerto Rico and its Municipalities. Puerto Rico Institute of Statistics, Accessed July 2024. https://censo.estadisticas.pr/node/499

[7]   Nydia Bauzá, "Historic low in the birth rate: fewer Puerto Ricans continue to be born on the island," Primera Hora. January 3, 2024. Accessed November 27, 2025. https://www.primerahora.com/noticias/government-politics/notes/historical-low-in-the-birth-rate-still-being-less-born-Puerto Ricans-on-the-island/

A figure that translates to 1 person in 69 worldwide; almost twice as many as a decade ago.[8]

Racism continues to show its ugly face. Cancel culture took its toll on society. And the growing tension between generations is becoming more and more evident. We have information overload. An avalanche of angry voices saturates social networks, full of cynicism and arrogance. To make matters worse, the pandemic has been followed by a crisis in mental health worldwide, which has raised the prevalence of anxiety and depression to 25%.[9]

WELCOME TO THE NEW NORMAL

There are two things that a V.U.C.A. environment will necessarily demand of all of us. The first is that we learn to serve as a team. Because to be honest, no leader is so intelligent, nor has the necessary experience to face everything that this new normal continues to throw at us. If someone tells you that he or she is indeed capable of doing so, don't believe it. What's more, if there is something really dangerous, it is when a person does not know that he does not know. Therefore,

[8]   Ala Kheir, "Global Trends Report". UNHCR, the UN Refugee Agency. June 1, 2024. Accessed November 27, 2024. Https://www.acnur.org/tendencias-globales
[9]   "The COVID-19 pandemic increases the prevalence of anxiety and depression worldwide by 25%." World Health Organization. March 2, 2022. Accessed November 27, 2024.
https://www.who.int/es/news/item/02-03-2022-covid-19-pandemic-triggers-25-increase-in-prevalence-of-anxiety-and-depression-worldwide

these times require us to learn to work as a team. And the second thing that these days demand of us is a corollary to the first: a lot of humility.

V.U.C.A. times unmask the illusion of our sense of control. But on most occasions, we are unable to appreciate such a gift. So we'll struggle not to sit still. What's more, it seems that even when attempting to stay still we can't stop moving. After all, we have been taught that we should be powerful, not weak, and proud rather than humble. But Sayers adds a note of hope for all those who come to appreciate the gift of identifying and accepting their many limitations, clinging to the very presence of God:

> "We have been taught by the great strongholds of our day, whether formed with a structure of secularism or cultural Christianity (or a hybrid of both), that pressure is a bad thing. That it is possible to live life and walk through the raindrops without getting wet. So as the cultural pressure increases...in our gray zone moment and we find ourselves in a wilderness, those who turn to God, who choose not to run from the wilderness, who seek His presence in the wilderness, will be transformed with spiritual authority".[10]

Those fears that make us feel inadequate gain a lot of ground in crises. So instinctively we will try to stop them as only we know how. Talking a lot, projecting ourselves as better informed than we are and moving a lot. Entertaining ourselves a lot; feeding ourselves more than necessary; occupying ourselves tirelessly; worrying a lot; and fighting like a cat on its

---

[10]   Mark Sayers, A Non-Anxious Presence: How a Changing and Complex World will Create a Remnant of Renewed Christian Leaders. (Chicago, IL: Moody Publishers, 2022), 181-182.

back to retain even the slightest illusion of control. And although we are always like this, crises manage to further exacerbate our great vulnerability, triggering fears, shame, traumas, insecurities, guilt and other emotional ailments. What does God expect from me, to remain in the desert, to have to look at and face all that?

We typically can't stand the silence of inactivity, preferring to embrace the raucous noise of activism. We are terrified of standing still in our own company, because that restless silence forces us to think about things we would rather forget or ignore. But that in no way means that we know what to do. And because we do not know how to keep silent or be still, we almost never know what, when, much less, how to act. That explains why it's often those most scared in any group who end up taking care of some of the most important decisions. Like when some disciples of Jesus, obviously upset, dare to advise him (as if He didn't know better): "Send the crowds away, so they can go to the villages and buy themselves some food".[11] We all know what Jesus opportunely did with that bad counsel, born of people controlled by their anxiety. However, even though I am ashamed to admit it, I would surely have suggested the same solution.

In fact, to discern what anxiety prevents us from detecting, we must first examine anxiety itself, beginning with its constant haste and deceptive negativity. We must also learn to think differently and not through opinion polls. The best decisions tend to come from people who think radically differently from the rest. It is precisely for that reason that they are there,

[11]   Mathew 14:13-21 NIV

or rather, that, in his merciful management, God put those people there.

TWO PRAYERS THAT MAKE A DIFFERENCE

Some of my worst crises have brought with them many valuable gifts that over the years I have learned to appreciate. I want to briefly share some of them with you.

- At the end of the day, what Jesus is looking for are followers rather than "leaders."
- If you let Him, God will show you the way.
- Those who lead from fear make bad decisions.
- Don't assume you have to save the day.
- Don't give in to the worst-case scenario mentality.
- You can do a lot without a building.
- You can make better use of your budget.
- Sharing a clear message from God is non-negotiable.
- People grow up in the wilderness, go through it with them.
- Life happens in the real world, join people there.
- You can anticipate that God will send new talent willing to help; give them permission to do so.
- People will be more open to consider a change than you expect.
- God specializes in redeeming suffering, don't ask Him for shortcuts, neither for yourself, nor for others.
- Remember, the best prayer is not the one that tells God what to do.
- The team is the new leader; and depending on God is the order of the day.

During the V.U.C.A. times caused by the COVID-19 crisis, two prayers by the apostle Paul on behalf of the Christians of Colossae, have been influencing mine. The first reads: "We ask God to give you complete knowledge of his will and to give you spiritual wisdom and understanding".[12] Facing a V.U.C.A. environment will necessarily imply continuous decision-making. Many of us have already begun to suffer from something called decision fatigue.[13] Especially when the information at hand is volatile, uncertain, complex and ambiguous. Think about it, such a request could not be more pertinent then—that God give us full knowledge of His will, so that we may always know what is best to do. "Then the way you live will always honor and please the Lord, and your lives will produce every kind of good fruit".[14] God wants to guide each of us, and if we let Him, that's precisely what He will do.

The second prayer reads: "We also pray that you will be strengthened with all his glorious power so you will have all the endurance and patience you need".[15] Were you able to see it? Endurance and patience, supernatural!

Pastor and psychologist, John Eldredge[16], explains that one of the most significant differences between camels and horses is that you can tell when a horse is tired, but not so with camels. The horse shows obvious signs of tiredness and thirst.

---

[12]   Colossians 1:9b NLT
[13]   Jon Johnson. "What is decision fatigue?", Medical News Today. July 7, 2020. Accessed November 27, 2024. Https://www.medicalnewstoday.com/articles/decision-fatigue
[14]   Colossians 1:10b NLT
[15]   Colossians 1:11 NLT
[16]   John Eldredge, Resilient: Restoring Your Weary Soul in These Turbulent Times. (Thomas Nelson, 2022), ix.

But the camel, at first glance, does not seem to get tired. This powerful animal can traverse entire deserts without showing any sign of tiredness or thirst. And that's precisely why when you least expect it to do so, but need the camel most, it can suddenly plummet. You can't depend on reading any signs of tiredness because it will never give them to you. So you have to give it water and rest, even if the camel never shows that it needs them.

Our problem is that you and I are like the camel. And, almost always, when faced with a crisis, we will throw ourselves into it until we solve it. After all, someone has to do it, right? We fight, we run, we charge, we decide, and... well, we already know the rest; that's who we are. Hence, often, even after we have reached the other side, and to everyone's surprise, we suddenly collapse.

We, just like the camel, do not allow ourselves to show signs of tiredness. Even less do we allow ourselves to stop and rest. Replenishing reserves seems illegal to many of us; especially before it's too late. That's why we burn the reserves until we literally have none left. And keep this in mind, no Sabbath will restore you from a burnout. The sabbatical should be taken much earlier, to avoid burning out, not to treat it[17]. Also, if your problem is the way you use your work time, you need to learn how to use that time better. Taking a break is insufficient, if when you return from your vacation, you return to the same way of using your time, then any reserve that your rest has replenished, will be consumed before the end of your first month

---

[17]   Robert C. Sales, Planning Sabbaticals: A Guide for Congregations and their Pastors. (Chalice Press, 2019), 6-7.

back. We can and must do better than that. Resilience is an act of preparation and not of pretense. A consequence of being in His Presence, and not of projecting cleverness. And in a world like ours, immersed in competition and speed, it is very difficult to develop that kind of resilience.

FOURTEEN — FOURTEEN — FOURTEEN

Genealogies have never been among the most widely read portions of the Bible, but this has been to our own detriment. Also, the following is not just any genealogy. Matthew writes:

> "This is a record of the ancestors of Jesus the Messiah, a descendant of David and of Abraham: Abraham was the father of Isaac. Isaac was the father of Jacob. Jacob was the father of Judah and his brothers. Judah was the father of Perez and Zerah (whose mother was Tamar). Perez was the father of Hezron. Hezron was the father of Ram. Ram was the father of Amminadab. Amminadab was the father of Nahshon. Nahshon was the father of Salmon. Salmon was the father of Boaz (whose mother was Rahab). Boaz was the father of Obed (whose mother was Ruth). Obed was the father of Jesse. Jesse was the father of King David. David was the father of Solomon (whose mother was Bathsheba, the widow of Uriah). Solomon was the father of Rehoboam. Rehoboam was the father of Abijah. Abijah was the father of Asa. Asa was the father of Jehoshaphat. Jehoshaphat was the father of Jehoram. Jehoram was the father of Uzziah. Uzziah was the father of Jotham. Jotham was the father of Ahaz. Ahaz was the father of Hezekiah. Hezekiah was the father of Manasseh. Manasseh was the father of Amon. Amon was the father of Josiah. Josiah was the father of Jehoiachin and his brothers (born at the time of the exile to Babylon). After the Babylonian exile: Jehoiachin was the father of Shealtiel. Shealtiel was the father of Zerubbabel. Zerubbabel was the father of Abiud. Abiud was the father

of Eliakim. Eliakim was the father of Azor. Azor was the father of Zadok. Zadok was the father of Akim. Akim was the father of Eliud. Eliud was the father of Eleazar. Eleazar was the father of Matthan. Matthan was the father of Jacob. Jacob was the father of Joseph, the husband of Mary. Mary gave birth to Jesus, who is called the Messiah. All those listed above include fourteen generations from Abraham to David, fourteen from David to the Babylonian exile, and fourteen from the Babylonian exile to the Messiah".[18]

Matthew uses a phrase that very well seems to pick up everything he wants to tell us in his first two chapters about the birth of Jesus. The phrase refers to the mighty king Herod and goes like this: "when Herod was mocked by the wise men." Clearly, what that phrase is really saying is, "When Herod was mocked by God." Well, if you think about it, the Magi are incidental, it is God who does it to Herod. Matthew's genealogy is a powerful argument for the same phenomenon, God circumventing obstacles and getting His way, regardless. Each name represents a human impossibility or a dead end. But still, God ends up serving Himself with the bigger spoon on every occasion.

The promised Messiah is born, not only in spite of so many setbacks, but through so many setbacks. When doing His things, God considers our gross failures and shameful sins. Even our accidents, if you can call them that. God also deals with our dead ends—from the infertility of Abraham and Isaac's wives respectively, to the tragic deaths of Naomi's husband, and two sons; from the establishment of the monarchy at its golden age under Solomon, to the shameful deportation

---

[18]   Matthew 1:1-17 NLT

to Babylon at its most desperate moments. Followed by the triumphant return from exile, which would finally be subsidized by none other than their own oppressors.

God gets his way against all odds. He does so by presiding over everything, and taking into account even the slightest supposed deviation from course. Every human decision, sin, and error ends up being a punctual part of God's eternal plan on the way to fulfilling His blessed promise. In reality, God's sovereignty is resisted and rebelled against, yet that does not succeed in rendering Him powerless or even taking Him by surprise. And as you read each name, reviewing its dramatic stories, you see one miracle after another, one generation after another.

The enormous accumulation of difficulties, accidents, sins, omissions, evils and errors of each story represented is obvious. No one should doubt that something greater than the sum of its parts is happening here. God mocking our impossibles. God keeping His promises.

Matthew underscores the unparalleled mathematical precision of all these stories. In the Hebrew mind, numbers were a precious literary device to convey messages.[19] Moreover, a careful reading of the psalms serves to convince us of the Jewish poet's legendary use of different types of parallelisms, terseness or conciseness, imagery and figurative language, repetition, acrostics and expression of deep emotions. Literary resources with which the author seeks to say something. There are, for example, the alphabetic psalms, which use

---

[19]   John H. Walton, Comentario del Contexto Cultural de la Biblia. Antiguo Testamento: El Trasfondo Cultural de Cada Pasaje del Antiguo Testamento. (El Paso, Texas, Editorial Mundo Hispano, 2004), 572.

letters of the Hebrew alphabet (at the beginning of each verse), so that when reading it you could identify the central message of the whole psalm. They were a work of art. Other Psalms use the resource of the acrostic, where the first letter of each verse forms the word that indicates the central theme of the psalm. An example of the alphabetic psalm is Psalm 119, which is divided, as many know, into 22 stanzas, according to the number of the letters of the Hebrew alphabet. In the original, each of the eight main lines of each stanza begins with the letter that gives it its name. And therefore its degree of difficulty is amazing. So all these literary resources served as a kind of magnet that attracts the reader's eye to itself. Resources that highlight the dramatic importance of the content transmitted.

I dare to emphasize that in the first chapter of Matthew, our author tries to help us appreciate what he has read in that other acrostic that only God in person could write. A numerical acrostic written throughout history. God alone! This is God at work. God writing us three times fourteen under our own noses, when none of us were even counting.

God is doing things that are beautiful, perfect, and timed to the second, in spite of everything! And I should add, through it all! Mathew does his math and his pulse trembles, and his soul softens, fourteen — fourteen — fourteen.

He notices that, in Hebrew, the name David has the numerical value of fourteen, and therefore the name David is written three times from Abraham to Jesus. So, based on all this, it could be said that "this genealogy of three groups of fourteen generations is a true Gospel of the King Messiah —

all of history has its eyes set on the One, whose throne will endure forever."[20]

We must not rely on this text to snuggle. This passage does not assure us that our particular story will always have the ending we desire. It is not about us, and that is certainly clear from the text. It is not my name that appears at the end of that genealogy, it is not even my genealogy, it's the Messiah's. And of course it is in our interest that it should be so, but not in the way we are badly accustomed to it being convenient for us. We want to believe that every story in the Bible is essentially about me, that God will bring me out of Egypt, that God will bring me back from exile, that God will make me reign, that God will come to my rescue every time, etc. But this is not essentially my story, it is His story. The good news is that in one way or another I am invited to be part of this story and that is why I have hope. He is the Messiah, but He is more than that, He is my Messiah!

Again, this first chapter of Matthew should take our breath away. Matthew has not even begun to talk about the incomparable facts and impeccable discourses of Jesus, and he has already managed to leave his audience speechless; just by sharing his genealogy with us. And what could be considered as the title of his Gospel (or at most its preamble), contains enough to show us that we should approach Jesus with our eyes wide open, taking care to pay the most solemn attention to whatever He has to say to us, to warn us, to mold us, but above all, to that which He may be pleased to give us.

---

[20]   Pope Benedict XVI, Jesus of Nazareth: The Infancy Narratives. (Random House LLC, 2012), 6.

I see here both a consolation and an invitation. Consolation, because it reminds me that God is often doing more in history, precisely when He appears to be doing less. He mocks the most strategic of the Herods with everything that from my myopic perspective looks like nothing but defeat and darkness. Nothing will stop Him from keeping His promises. It is true, I read here consolation, but also an invitation. An invitation to realize God. An invitation to discern our times, in the light of the Gospel, and not based on fear and the lies of the world, and even less of the prince of this world.

Genealogies are especially valuable for people in exile. They served as a family album that perpetuates their story. They literally saved entire villages from being obliterated. Even in the midst of exile, when nothing seems to make sense, and one's own identity seems to hang by a thread. We remember that this story has not just begun with us, and that it is much bigger than us. And in this hard exile, the invitation is to not forget who we are; and to celebrate that we have not been forgotten.

Let us pause then to interpret our actuality, but let's do so in light of that God. I think we will then see and understand everything in a completely different way. One of the most powerful things God has taught me in recent years is to review the course of my life over decades. It is impressive what one begins to discover from God. God doesn't waste an Alzheimer's, or a hurricane, or a divorce, or a widowhood, or a prodigal son, or a pandemic, or a new friend, or a new baby, or an evangelical denomination.

Take a breath, God is mocking and occupying all our Herods. But if we don't stop to interpret what happens to us with God's help, believe me, then someone else will misinterpret our life for us. We are living historic days; and I pray to God that you will receive new breath, remembering that God specializes in days such as this. God is at work and nothing and no one will be able to stop Him.

In 1939, as the clouds of war darkened over Europe, King George VI inspired countless human hearts through a Christmas message conveyed to the British Empire when he quoted these verses from a poem by Minnie Louise Haskins: "I said to the man at the door of the year: Give me a light that I may walk into the unknown." He answered, "Enter into the darkness and put your hand in God's hand. That will be better than light and safer than the known."[21] God Himself must be our new normal.

---

[21]   ""The Door of the Year" is the popular name given to a poem by Minnie Louise Haskins. The title given by the author was "God knows."

Javier Gómez Marrero

Chapter 2

Three Natural Enemies of Our Flourishing

"... pinch of clay, don't you know how little love you can have...".

— Francis Thompson
English poet, 1859-1907

Elie Wiesel, a famous survivor of the Nazi death camps, wrote the following story:

"One day a just man—young, vibrant, dynamic—decided that he must save the city of Sodom, the epitome of sin and deceit. So, he began going from street to street, from marketplace to marketplace. "Men and women," he said, "do not steal. Men and women, do not lie, do not sin." In the beginning people stopped to listen because he was amusing. After all, how many just men came to Sodom? But after a while he repeated himself so much that they stopped listening. After many years, he was so old that he could hardly walk, yet he was walking every morning, going from street to street, from marketplace to marketplace, and saying, "People, you are destroying yourselves. Repent. Remember God." Nobody listened. Then one little child stopped the man and said, "Poor stranger, poor teacher, why do you do all that? Don't you see that it's useless?" "Yes," said the old man. "Then why do you continue?" And the old teacher said, "I will tell you why, my son. In the beginning when I came here, I was convinced that I would manage to change them. Now I know I will never change them. But if I continue and I shout louder and louder and I scream more and more, it is because I don't want them to change me".[22]

How close have you already been to embracing that chronic hopelessness, which seems to be enveloping everything today? I suppose you've at least flirted with a feeling of apathy, that persuasive idea that we shouldn't even waste time trying to do something about anything. And if not, perhaps you have wondered, will something ever go right, finally? I do, and more times than I would like to admit.

But then I remember the Gospel. "Do not conform to the pattern of this world but be transformed by the renewing of your mind. Then you will be able to test and approve what God's will is—his good, pleasing and perfect will".[23] In just one verse, the Apostol Paul succeeds in contrasting the precarious history of mankind, which he prefers to call "this world," with God's magnificent dream for that very humanity. A dream that Paul refers to as the good will of God, pleasing and perfect. Thus laying the groundwork to help us appreciate the incredible flourishing that the God of the Gospel longs for us.

The ideal of God! That extraordinary way of being, living and doing, which evidently distances itself abysmally from

---

[22]   2016. Elie Wiesel. "A Last Breath of Witness". Y Magazine, Fall 2016 Issue.https://magazine.byu.edu/article/elie-wiesel-last-breath-witness/
[23]   Romans 12:2 NIV

our desperate and common experience of reality. An ideal that our predictable twisted way of thinking miserably sabotages over and over again without even trying.

Paul has much more to say about that twisted way of thinking in the verses that follow from that revealing twelfth chapter of Romans. We typically only read up to verse two, so we mistakenly conclude that renewing our understanding aims only at learning something, thus reducing the potential transformation of the Christian person to the simple act of acquiring new information. We reach this conclusion, at least in part, because we also reduce that good, pleasant and perfect will of God to purely circumstantial things. Things in the order of: where does God want me to work or when does God want me to settle down? Rather than referring to: how will God want us to live, or what kind of person and society does He want us to be? And especially: how does He intend to achieve this?

ANOTHER WAY OF THINKING

But if you manage to get to verse three, you will see that the renewal of understanding encompasses much more than the mere act of acquiring new information. Paul writes: "For I say, through the grace that was given me, to every man that is among you, not to think of himself more highly than he ought to think; but so to think as to think soberly, according as God hath dealt to each man a measure of faith".[24] For to advance towards such an ideal, which is God's desire, is not merely to learn something. It also requires, especially, adopting

---

[24]   Romans 12:3 ASV

a new way of thinking about reality,[25] that is akin to the revolutionary implications of the work and person of Jesus.

Paul teaches that man tries to live in a universe that is not even there. A universe where people can supposedly define themselves and become self-sufficient. Illusory pretense is just the tip of the iceberg. For human beings have even come to suppose themselves capable of altering, and of adjusting, reality itself as they see fit. Instead of needing to explore it as the glorious mystery that we have all been invited to enjoy, to respect, and especially to take care of.

In his argument, Paul uses two expressions that stand out: rational and sanity. The first appears when, after having shared with us eleven chapters saturated with the Gospel, Paul invites us to do the only thing that would be rational to do: center our whole lives on the powerful author of that glorious Gospel. "Which is your reasonable service",[26] the apostle tells us enthusiastically. His second expression alludes to the only sane way of thinking, as a result of the truth of the Gospel. Paul knows that until our thinking is grounded in the Gospel, little will begin to change in us. For, in order to try to survive in our exile from paradise, we have necessarily embraced a notion of ourselves that bears no relation to reality. And, like the rest, we will end up living according to the social imaginary[27]

---

[25]   One way of thinking about reality is something known as a mental map.

[26]   Romans 12:1

[27]   The social imaginary consists of a set of social assumptions, which represent a type of consensus during a given cultural moment. It's the way we instinctively assume things are, even if we don't know how we came to that conclusion or why. For example: science is the only source

of our respective historical moment, conforming to (i.e., taking the form of) this century, including its elaborate inconsistencies about what leads to authentic human flourishing. Thus, distancing us from reality and doing so at full gallop.

So, our very lives hang on that phrase, "think of yourself with sober judgment, in accordance with the faith God has distributed to each of you".[28] How can we even begin to think according to the Gospel, and therefore with sanity? For that I will refer to you Jesus' brilliant Parable of the Sowers.[29] A parable with which Jesus addresses the different reactions to his message, according to the only four possible ways of thinking within our reach. I propose here that the first three represent the strategies for flourishing that humanity has promoted, under different names, throughout history. While the fourth terrain represents the one strategy for flourishing we could not come up with on our own and is the only one that leads to our true flourishing.

The first three depend on us pretending to be more than mere human beings, which seems essential if we want to survive outside of paradise. Because the more apparent fangs and claws we have, the better your chances will be. And yet, remember this well: surviving is not flourishing. But, in the absence of the Gospel, you have no choice but to make use of popular wisdom. The "wisdom" that through its powerful advertising machine will try to convince you of the "truth" of one

---

of truth; the human being is essentially good; as a society we are progressing; truth is relative; it cannot be a sin if fate wills it; if you want you can achieve anything; it doesn't matter what you believe as long as you are sincere; winning is what counts; etc.

28   Romans 12:3 NIV
29   Mathew 13:1-23

of three lies, which I will call here the three natural enemies of our flourishing: (1) Trust no one (create yourself) — a false identity. (2) Listen to your heart (embrace your own truth)—a false faith. (3) Escape reality (avoid, or medicate, your pain) — a false god.

TRUST NO ONE

In a life lived far from paradise, our natural habitat, we will all face our fears as best we can. Especially the most primitive fears, such as shame and fear of dying. When it comes to trying to face our fears, popular wisdom advises that the best way is to trust no one. This results in defining ourselves for ourself, beyond what others, and especially society as a whole, may want to impose upon us. This transforms us into people who aspire to have full autonomy.

Our self-definition will include those aptitudes, desires, opinions, strengths and weaknesses that we have been discovering in ourself. In practice, the goal will be to convince not only ourself of your self-definition, but also the next person we come across. We are then faced with one of the most unusual contradictions of which we are capable as a society, since this supposed self-definition necessarily depends on the validation of others. So, while it is true that this proposal arose as an understandable reaction to the use and abuse of the social practice of labeling each other, we are unable to free ourselves form it. At the end of the day, we expect and need someone else to read and validate the label we have decided to put on ourselves in order to feel safe. Thus, we end up defending the freedom to be authentic[30], meaning to disregard all inhibitions, accusing others of hypocrisy or the freedom to be sincere[31], meaning that what I do must correspond to the identity I have decided to forge, accusing others of inconsistency. In either case, always needing validation from the same society we criticize, because no human being can exist strictly on his own account. It is other human beings, by recognizing me[32] and dealing with me, that make my own existence a concrete reality. Otherwise, it's as if I didn't exist. That's why the worst insult that can be committed against any person is not to offend them, but to make them invisible.

As Carl R. Trueman explains very well:

> "Individual identity is thus truly a dialogue: how a person thinks of himself is the result of learning the language of the community so that he can be a part of the community. It also explains the basic human need to belong: the idea of the isolated Rousseauesque man of nature, living all by himself and for himself, may be superficially attractive, but a moment's reflection would indicate how strange, if not completely absurd, it would be."[33]

Therefore, in the absence of the Gospel — and therefore lacking the definitive dialogue with the One who is the

---

[30]   Carl R. Trueman, The Origin and Triumph of the Modern Ego. (Eerdmans, 2020), 61.
[31]   Adam Grant. "Be yourself is bad advice." The New York Times. June 9, 2026. Accessed November 27, 2024. https://www.nytimes.com/es/2016/06/09/espanol/opinion/se-tu-mismo-es-un-pesimo-consejo.html?smid=url-share
[32]   Carl R. Trueman, The Origin and Triumph of the Modern Ego. (Eerdmans, 2020), 81.
[33]   Ibid, 69-70.

Word — we will need society to dialogue with us our identity. Whether society wants to impose an identity on us, or we want to impose our self-definition on society, we would still be participating in an inferior dialogue, with our resulting identity always in question and, necessarily, on the defensive.

Today, we prefer to define ourselves rather than leave that job to some incompetent or even worse to those who could take advantage of us. Everything seems to point to the fact that society has already made peace with that state of affairs, placing that heavy burden on each individual. This explains much of the collective anxiety that characterizes us today. In the absence of the Gospel, it would only remain for us to wish you the best of good luck with that impossible enterprise of creating yourself.

Do you know how to make people laugh? Or is your thing to lead, or cook; or none of the above? Perhaps you are skilled with logical thinking, or are artistic or athletic, or not. Maybe intelligence is prominent in you or wisdom. Have you mastered the art of persuasion, or developed charisma, or express yourself well in public? Would you rather be swallowed up by the earth than speaking in public? You may be exceptionally good at what you do for a living, or you may be average. Maybe you've accomplished some of the things that society validates as success, or none of them. All of those weaknesses, strengths, experiences, and opinions that you or your parents have defended (because sometimes even these are inherited), become your way of defining yourself, of presenting yourself to the world in the continuous search for its coveted validation. Because you don't really know who you are or at least are not sure enough, that constant insecurity steals your life. It will inevitably end up turning you into a defensive and reactionary person, because your own sense of identity will always be at stake. A life that in no way can be considered an abundant life.

LISTEN TO YOUR HEART

The second lie arises from defective thought patterns resulting from what has already happened to us and affecting our interpretation of what is now happening to us. The same absurd premise that caused the downfall of our ancestors—the thought that they could act in God's place—makes us see the heart as the exclusive repository of ultimate truth.

"Listen to your heart" has become the new cultural norm that is supposed to make us flourish. A responsibility that is too big for the heart, so that listening to it will only lead you astray. For the heart seldom advises from a decision of which it is necessarily aware. Many of our ideas end up working behind the scenes. Some whisper to us; others shout at us, but we do not necessarily know from where, or from when, they come. "Dad was never home; Nobody wants to be with me." "Mom praised my good grades; I'm only worth something if I get good grades." Many conclusions that our hearts have reached are blind spots for us. Like other conclusions that we do come to notice, these also operate as values that translate into behavior, and eventually, of course, into personal culture. Basically, our heart tells us, "That's always the way things are around here." So it is that our way of being is much more automated and based on our past than we would like to believe.

These defective thought patterns form a kind of creed, with which we define the contour and content of our reality. Believing then only what we want or suppose it convenient to come to believe. Therefore, pragmatism will be the order of the day, and personal comfort the only constant measure. But in the end, even if it sounds attractive, that does not lead to freedom from fear, and even less to a flourishing life.

ESCAPE FROM REALITY

The third lie arises from the attempt to alleviate, numb or manage the pain of living in a reality that is painful, dangerous and treacherous. We think anything that manages to relieve or distract us from the distressing reality of the human condition will serve us well. Especially if it helps us escape from ourselves. This materialistic society has stripped life of transcendence and meaning. It takes away the will to live of anyone who stops long enough to consider the implications of it. So we prefer not to stop. Much less think. Perhaps that is the worst pandemic of this time, our collective renunciation of thinking for ourselves.

Recreational drugs and alcohol could be the symbols of our search for escape, as they represent that continuous search for an alternate reality. A fantasy reality that is willing to welcome us with open arms, and that allows us to escape from the one that has apparently closed its arms to us. A parallel reality that in some multi-verse would always allow us to get our way.

The invitation to avoid pain at all costs always looks very seductive. Still, we know that trying to make life tolerable is not enough. We want to control it minute by minute. We want to extirpate all suffering from it. We want rights without duties. We want instant satisfaction. We want laughter without tears. We want to mature, but only by taking care of ourselves. We want to help, but only if someone sees us. We want freedom to decide, but also to free ourselves from the consequences of our bad decisions. We want to repent, but not of our sins. We want the kingdom of God, but without God.

Everything we use and opportunely abuse to escape, will always assume the form of an idol that will cruelly enslave us. Because an idol is like an addiction, and every addiction is a kind of slavery. They always dehumanize us, generating the most terrible destruction. And every idol always begins as something else; such as a job, career, hobby, or relationship. But over time we begin to see it as a source from which we can at least pretend to derive the identity and security that in reality only God can give us. Therefore, even some of the least threatening addictions can become as destructive as those that we consider extremely harmful. So it's impossible to list the potential idols at our disposal because of their great number, as well as their incredible diversity. Not to mention how quickly they continue growing in a society that is friendly to the ideals and premises of its idols.

So, all secular wisdom boils down to three lies: (1) Trust no one (create yourself), which results in a false identity. (2) Listen to your heart (embrace your truth), which results in false faith. (3) Escape from reality (avoid, or medicate, your pain), which is nothing more than a false god. But there is another wisdom. And even the least wise aspect about it is much wiser than ours.[34]

---

[34]   I Corinth 1:25

Chapter 3

It Couldn't Have Occurred to Us

"… spiritual formation has less to do with erecting an edifice of knowledge than with the development of a Christian know-how that intuitively understands the world in the light of the Gospel."

— James K. Smith
Philosopher and theologian
Canadian-American

Speaking of this Christian know-how, do you remember what, according to Jesus, distinguishes the last soil from the other three in the Parable of the Sower?

Understanding the Gospel message![35]

All soils represent different things, but they all have something in common. And it is that each of them represents those who heard the message of truth. So, they all have that in common, that they could hear; all had genuine access to the truth. But it is of the fourth soil that we are told represents those who not only heard but also understood the truth. That is the only soil from which a harvest finally sprouts. A great harvest! Biblically, understanding is not just a cognitive act, it's wisdom. It is to put into practice the truth until it opportunely does its thing in us.

---

[35]   Mathew 13:23

To be good soil implies, then, not only to be a forgetful hearer of the truth, but a doer of the truth.[36] It means avoiding the conditions of the other three fields, which always end up rejecting, confusing or forgetting the truth. By receiving it and practicing it, we can benefit abundantly from the results.

RENOUNCING THE ME-IST[37] PROJECT

In the case of the first soil, in which the seed does not even manage to penetrate its hard surface[38], becoming a good soil will require the categorical renunciation of the me-ist project.

Pastor Jon Tyson writes about it:

"Augustine called this preoccupation with the self *"Incurvatus."* Love turned in on itself. Commenting on this, Jeff Cook writes, *"The more I make my life, my well-being, my enlightenment, and my success primary, the farther I step from reality. Thus, the hell-bound do not travel downward; they travel inward, cocooning themselves behind a mass of vanity, personal rights, religiosity, and defensiveness. Obsession with self is the defining mark of a disintegrating soul."* Paul warned that the end times would be terrible because people would be *"lovers of themselves"*.[39]

---

36   James 1:22 RV1960
37   Me-me-me as in "it's all about me".
38   "When anyone hears the word of the kingdom and does not understand it, the wicked one comes and snatches away what was sown in his heart." — Matthew 13:23 KJV1960
39   Jon Tyson. "The Spiritual Progress Your Heart Longs For". Jon Tyson Archive. Accessed November 27, 2024. https://jontysonarchive.com/jon-tyson-archive/blog-post-title-one-wpmwe-x6arh-9e4fb-39tjr-h6kmn-g4x9c-t9tgg-f6fh9-psybz-myltd-sks34-fbzc6?rq=The%20Spiritual%20Progress%20Your%20Heart%20Longs%20For.

Ironically, pretending to define yourself prevents you from being your true self and ends up being exploitative, unfair, and cruel. Creating an identity is a never-ending project that is continually threatened. It's only a matter of time, but sooner or later it will swallow you alive.

That is why Paul warns that having a concept of oneself that is higher than it should be is debilitating. Because of my own self-absorption, each of my problems becomes the most important in the world, making my existence a crushing experience.

Curiously, what we most need to understand is that we are not the protagonist of this story. We actually play a secondary role, as do our problems. A self-perception that fits that reality is at the very heart of a healthy and fulfilling life.

It's true, there's such a thing as a real you. But when we talk about the real you, we are not referring to characteristics, opinions, desires, experiences and qualities, which, although important, do not define you. We're talking about the person you were created to be. We are referring to the immense intrinsic dignity with which you were graced when you were given being and to that relationship that really makes you be who you are—your relationship with God.

The real you is not something you can produce but only recognize and receive. Something that, of course, you can cultivate, and encourage, realizing its potential to mature. I'm not referring to a static you that can't grow, but a seed that can develop to its full potential. The self-centered person that this harsh world has turned you into is not the real you. The expensive costume that others want to sell you, and that you want to buy, or produce yourself, is not you. That powerful invisible force field with which you shield yourself, is not you. It is rather the most recent form of slavery of the modern human being. Like all slavery, it dehumanizes you and cries out for a liberator. Still, that is the person many see themselves as. That's the way many present themselves to the world, as well as their main survival strategy. All the while, they stumble forward under the constant, and stabbing, feeling of inconsistency.

In a world that is not even a shadow of what it should be, it is easy to understand the secrecy with which we cling to our sophisticated fig leaves.[40] The ones that become so familiar to us that we all confuse them with our identity, but we are not that person. Sadly, the real self is so insecure and ashamed that it fights for cover with tooth and claw, masquerading behind a charade that gradually replaces it. For that reason, no one knows the real person; not even oneself.

But that defensive posture is not the way out, however tempting it may be. Listening to understand and learn, not to defend oneself, is. That is why the word repentance, which is the one with which Jesus introduces his good news, takes on the greatest importance. This comes from the Greek metanoia and means change of mind; and therefore, implies a change of agenda. This makes a lot of sense, since being able to differ from oneself and concede the possibility of being wrong, is where all potential change and all true personal transformation begins.

If always being right is what we assume will make us feel safe, then we will continue to build a false identity behind which we intend to hide. A false self that shelters us because

---

[40]   Genesis 3:7

we do not feel safe yet. And that fear can only mean one thing, that we have not yet met perfect love.[41]

This is why we are often unable to revise our positions, or even to admit our doubts. And when that happens, then an old enemy formerly represented as a deceitful serpent, now arrives like a hungry bird devouring the valuable seed that our hard and stubborn soil despised.

THE MOST DECEPTIVE THING OF ALL

In the case of the second soil, in which the seed is unable to grow deep due to the stones that block its path, becoming a good soil implies realizing that the heart is deceitful. So, in no way should we allow it to be in charge of defining our reality by instilling false ideas in us.

Such ideas leave little visible trace of what the wounds are, and the people or situations from which those wounds come, but you need to identify them and replace them with the truth. Especially when every faulty reasoning hidden in us becomes like a huge building. Not a passing idea that by just shaking your head you will be able to erase, but rather well-rooted ideas that will resist defeat, like buildings with solid foundations. It is precisely this deep foundation that explains their great strength.

These are ideas that you will not be able to knock down without help. That help is a person. Someone who did something of such magnitude that, if you make it your truth, it will

---

[41]   1 John 4:18

tear down old ideological edifices that populate your being. In-cluding lofty structures built years ago on the fallacies of a quasi-religious, earthly, common sense. A destruction of false ideas essential to any Christian discipleship worth its salt.

Paul put it like this: "We take captive every thought to make it obedient to Christ".[42] In the Gospel, such obedience never refers to the effort of human nature to appear presenta-ble. Trying to be accepted for fulfilling the law is not good news, but the cruelest slavery. The same one from which the Gospel comes to free us.

To obey Christ is rather to listen to what God says through the Son, to take it for granted, and to act accordingly. It is, therefore, to embrace the reality that is there, as it is there, because it is there. One does not proceed to sit in a chair, with-out assuming that the chair to be used will support the weight. That is, one does not make an effort when sitting down to test every chair one sits on, instead one simply sets all the weight down on the chair. Likewise, faith hears and obeys, acting ac-cordingly. If it doesn't, it's not genuine faith.

Therefore, if God is telling us that he loves us uncon-ditionally, we should obey that truth.

Obeying the truth of that unconditional love could sometimes be seen as keeping silent. For example, if someone criticizes or dislikes me, keeping silent would be a concrete way of living in the real world, enjoying the fact that, thanks to God's love, I am now free from the opinion of others. Instead of continuing to reinforce the hard servitude of having to ex-plain myself to that other person or of having to convince that

---

[42]   2 Corinthians 10:5 NIV

other person every time; I would be reinforcing my precious freedom. To obey God is to acknowledge that what He is telling me is the truth. That being so, the only manner in which to act is to place all my weight fall freely on that truth.

Obeying is the freedom to live in reality; and not in our twisted version of it. Trusting and experiencing the truth, and not just knowing it, is what sets us free.[43] Especially since acting according to the truth is what breaks the bonds of our muscle memory, not only the memory of our material muscles, but also of our spiritual ones.

Because it is not enough to assert the truth, it is also necessary to experience the effective power of the truth practiced in the real world. One thing I often do is give myself permission to act out the truth in very practical ways, such as taking deep breaths. I can say something like: "Take a deep breath Javier, because Jesus has already made your rest possible; calmly focus on your breathing because you no longer need to get lost in hundreds of tasks; rest because thanks to Jesus you can stop, in him you lack nothing else."

Rick Lawrence, writing about how the stories we tell ourselves determine the way we function and influence our limitations and possibilities, says:

> "Dan McAdams, a professor of psychology at Northwestern University, calls this our "narrative identity"—it's our own personal mythology, complete with plot twists, thematic threads, and heroes and villains. McAdams says we tell ourselves two basic self-narratives: 1) Redemptive Stories, and 2) Contamination Stories. The first kind of story is transplanted

---

[43]   John 8:31-32

from the Kingdom of God, where redemption is not only the mission of the Messiah, but also the heartbeat of life. The second kind of story is exported and propagated by the Kingdom of Darkness, where "killing, stealing and destroying" (John 10:10) is the mission".[44]

So, following the trail of lies until we identify their foundation, and replace them with the truth, alters the story we end up telling ourselves. Because it is not the same to be telling ourselves "I am a burden to everyone", "I never do anything right", "I always end up spoiling everything I do"; things that we would never say to a friend, but that we are always saying to ourselves; than instead begin to tell ourselves the fundamental truth about who we are now in light of the event and the person of Jesus.

Human beings will always need to strive to understand what is happening in their lives. The idea of a meaningless life is intolerable to us. That's why it's so hard for us to let the "blank spaces" pass, that portion of the narrative that is unfolding in real time right before us, but of which we do not know many details.

"Why didn't he greet me, it must be because he is angry with me." "So-and-so told me that he wants to meet with me; it must be because he wants to hold me accountable for something I don't even remember doing." "I may have done something that offended her." "Peter has not answered my text message; it must be because he is ignoring me."

---

[44]   Rick Lawrence, "Vibrant faith". Why God leaves weeds in our story. (Article - August 10, 2024).

We rush to fill in the blanks with the only thing we really have, not facts, but pure conjectures. No wonder we end up with so many misunderstandings. From the most trivial to the most significant detail is subject to multiple interpretations.

But what happens when this interpretation does not align with reality, as so often happens? Nothing good. Like a stone that occupies the place that a seed would have benefitted from. By believing ourselves capable of reading the minds of others, our destructive conjectures blocks spaces where a humble "help me understand" would have opened up the way for the truth.

The same happens with even more serious matters, such as those that involve many of the most significant and transcendental perspectives and decisions of our lives. We all tend to create our respective version of reality, and we always lean towards the version that helps us appear in the best light possible.

The parable of the prodigal son portrays a younger son who is convinced that he will do better away from the father; and so, leaving, he spends everything.[45] While the eldest son conjectures that he will do better by winning over his father with his good conduct; and so, staying, he spends nothing.

The first son gambles his life on questionable behavior, and the other on honorable behavior. One chooses to live the wildlife, and the other the restrained life. But neither chooses to live in actual reality, because they cannot live with themselves. So, they both hide from the light. The younger will be unhappy among pigs and husks, and the elder will be unhappy

---

45   Luke 15:11-32

among fatted calves. Neither manages to recognize, much less receive, the love and abundance of the father. So, neither flourishes... until one of them finally comes to his senses, thereby exposing the most deceitful thing of all: his own heart.

OUR BEAUTIFUL LIES OR THE TRUTH

In Luke 14:25-35, Jesus offers three vivid illustrations of the grave danger of acting on what some sociologists refer to as "the beautiful lie" of our favorite narrative, instead of facing the truth. The first scene consists of a bricklayer who admits that he does not have the necessary resources to build his house. So, wisely, he decides to avoid even laying the first brick. The second is about a king who admits that he does not have the necessary soldiers to win the war. So, prudently, he decides to avoid the war and instead negotiates peace. The third scene features a merchant who realizes that his abundant inventory of salt has all been spoiled. Therefore, wisely, he chooses to desist from all types of commercial use, recognizing that his only option is to cast it out.

The three scenes allude to the importance of coming to terms with a deficit that is painfully significant, but at the same time will shed light on the only possible way forward. Instead of trying to convince ourselves of a beautiful lie. How much more important then will it be to come to terms with our infinite shortcomings, beginning with the one we are most ashamed of, our deficit of righteousness? Will we courageously face the truth? The good news of the Gospel is that Jesus's righteousness becomes ours when we consent to it. And when that truth penetrates the subsoil of our soul, expropriating each and every lie, we'll get the most bountiful of harvests.

THE FRAUDULENT CHARM OF IDOLS

Dispensing with the third soil implies understanding that every idol is a fraud; no matter how large the immense number of people who are currently serving it may be. A dynamic that is not surprising, since what is constantly repeated, not only programs an automatic response, but also incites a persuasive vision of what flourishing looks like. Especially if the surrounding culture itself has already adopted such idea of flourishing. And we know that one will become, for better or worse, whatever it is that one has visualized. That's how the heart is captivated, and whatever has the attention of your heart, will have your money, energies, time, etc.

Fortunately, we have also begun to understand that our respective towns, villages and cities are not merely neutral spaces in which human life passes without much novelty. Each of these spaces, having immense and varied opportunities to speak to our imagination, become significant formative experiences and as such powerful enterprises of spiritual formation. They transmit and sculpt ideas, ideals, narratives, desires, and worldviews, not only in our imagination, but in our feelings, relationships, and even in our muscle memory. In other words, our villages and cities end up giving us a certain shape, even if we are not aware of it. Historically, each society has erected temples to its respective gods.[46] Today, those temples would include banks, universities, coliseums, shopping malls, theaters, digital spaces, and news conglomerates.

The philosopher and theologian James K. A. Smith, referring to the behavior linked to such structures, coined the instructive term secular liturgies.[47] Thus attributing to all kinds of public activity characteristics related to religious devotion. This includes activities such as saluting the flag, cheering for the home team, shopping, expressing admiration for an artist, and many other such activities. They communicate symbols, certain notions of good and evil, historical figures, acts of heroism, legends and narratives about reality. And no one is completely immune to its pervasive and seductive influence.

It has been said, rightly, that "everyone worships, the only choice we have is what to worship."[48] Even if we choose not to worship, the very "secular liturgy" we breathe will cause us to do so, even if casually and involuntarily.

Even today's partisan politics would seem to have become a kind of religion, occupying space and using the proselytizing practices for which religious institutions were once known. So, while it is true that church attendance has been declining lately, attendance at other types of meetings, identification with a related group, participation in some kind of common mission, and even community service has not. What used

---

[46]   James K. Smith, Desiring the Kingdom: Worship, Worldview and Cultural Formation. (Baker Academic, 2009), 9.
[47]   Ibid, 24.
[48]   David Foster Wallace. "This is Water". David Foster Wallace's 2005 commencement speech to the graduating class at Kenyon College. Farnam Street Media Inc. Downloaded on November 27, 2024. https://fs.blog/david-foster-wallace-this-is-water/

to take place exclusively in relation to a temple and its mission, it is now expressed in political rallies and in activities derived from their mission.

So, in one way or another, the city is eager to provide the same thing the people used to look for in the temple. To do so, each city has more advanced technology, bigger budgets, better buildings, and more members than any particular religious institution will ever have.

Now, my goal in telling you all this is not to stop you from going to the mall or the concert. My aim is to help you consider, as James K. Smith does, the enormous formative power of our habits.[49] Not only those we do in private, but all of them. So you can begin to ponder what effect all those practices have been having on you because of your habitual, though often unnoticed, exposure to them. For example, it is true that going to see a movie does not make you a promoter of all its ideas. But you should not forget that all its ideas are being promoted by the movie and you are the audience.

I once heard a pastor say that when he started watching movies with his children, he was concerned about their subtle, but at the same time obvious, ways of indoctrination. So he decided to invent a game that would allow them to enjoy the film without falling prey to its underlying ideology. The game consisted of trying to identify those ideas that were implied, or sponsored, by the film but that clashed head-on with their

---

[49]   James K. Smith, Desiring the Kingdom: Worship, Worldview and Cultural Formation. (Baker Academic, 2009), 10.

Christian worldview, and they had to say it out loud, thus identifying it as a lie. The one who identified the most lies was the winner.

For example, in the middle of a movie, someone might say something like "What that person is saying is the central idea of the philosophy of consumerism, there it is, but that is a lie because life does not consist of the abundance of goods that one possesses." After a while, another person might say something like, "What's implicit in what just happened in that scene is the central idea of individualism, there it is, but that's just a vile lie because human beings are dependent on God and interdependent on each other." And so subsequently, they would gain an increasing awareness of their vision of flourishing, vis-à-vis that of the world around them, consciously rejecting the latter. In addition, they did not even have to stop watching the films they wanted to see. Thus recovering a part of the public square that the secular liturgy gloats about daily and wisely including it in their own diet of Christian formation, instead of being limited exclusively to the temple.

EVERYTHING IS SACRED

According to the 10 commandments,[50] Everything in life is sacred: work, relationships, rest, marriage, time, sex, etc. So, contrary to what has surely been suggested to you, nothing is strictly secular. A 'strictly private faith' is a contradiction of terms. Our values and beliefs resist staying at home. Whatever anyone deems to be the real, the moral, and the beautiful will

---

[50]   Exodus 20:1-17

inform their mindset when it comes to walking in a park, dining at a restaurant, and having fun on game day. And on bridges, avenues, schools, shops, squares, etc. The question is not whether we will practice any spiritual discipline out in the world, but which ones we practice, and more importantly, what identity and notion of flourishing will these disciplines instill in us.

Secular liturgies always end up creating idols. If what we look for in these idols is something they can never give us, sooner or later they will take their toll on us. Those public liturgies have been contributing to our vision of flourishing; and therefore, also to our identity, continuously influencing our decisions, relationships, reasoning, and reactions. The more we keep that in mind, the more sense things will make and the more prepared we will be for the future. Believe me, we are no longer blocks of clay waiting to be formed for the first time, there has already been a lot of training, and also a lot of deformation, taking place in our lives, sometimes referred to as the empty way of life handed down to us from our ancestors.[51] Becoming aware of this needs to be part of any new training effort to be undertaken. Especially if it is to result in the kind of life that truly succeeds in flourishing.

---

[51]   1 Peter 1:18

Javier Gómez Marrero

PART II:

WHERE DO YOU COME FROM, WHERE ARE YOU GOING?

Javier Gómez Marrero

Chapter 4

That Which We Are Looking For

*"Of course, there's a healthy kind of side hustle where your life is
full of things that matter, not wasted on empty leisure
or trivial searches."*

— John Mark Comer
Renowned American
author and pastor

"Challenging the Geniuses" was a television comedy
that Puerto Rican audiences loved and sponsored for several
decades. It was made up of three or four "geniuses" who, assisted by a moderator, would try to guess a secret topic about
which they would supposedly receive only a tiny clue. Of
course, the viewer would know the subject in advance. During
each program and from comic occurrences, one genius after
another would come close to finding the subject almost to the
point of ridiculousness; only to be grossly sidetracked at the
last second, which made it laughably evident that they were anything but geniuses. The catchy phrase that was repeated
throughout the television episode was: "That which we are
looking for...!" The one phrase that, on the lips of one of the
most famous geniuses of the program, the beloved character
"Mister Bloop", made many laugh. As far as I remember, the
geniuses never found what they were looking for.

They say that the most successful comedies are those that tend to reflect reality. Our laughter reveals just how much we see ourselves portrayed in them. Possibly because our own search has not been as great, or as successful, as we all wish it has been. Is that why, according to the Gospels, the first question Jesus asks those who first showed interest in following him was: "What do you seek?"[52] I don't think there is a question that can better address the continuous comings and goings of all human struggles. It must be that we are all looking for something, but we don't even know what it is or where to find it.

INSATIABLE PEOPLE

One of the most apparent contradictions of the human condition is that we don't seem to know what it is that we really want. Even when we think we have already found it, we feel again that same thirst that drove us to seek it, and almost always with more strength. Jesus' question, in many ways, will haunt us throughout our lives. Sometimes, it will even frighten us, since it shows how little we know ourselves and the nature of our thirst; and because we can't stop until we quench it. Such an anguishing existential contradiction affects us to the deepest fiber of our being. In the words of the poet: "My soul thirsts... in dry and arid land, where there is no water."[53]

Our new normal is being characterized by people who feel deeply dissatisfied, and who seek to quench their thirst,

---

[52]   John 1:38 NKJV
[53]   Psalms 63:1b NIV

where there is no water. That insatiable search describes every moment we spend awake as people who are bored, anxious, depressed, chronically isolated, and unable to sleep without the help of medication[54]. Well, sadly, it has also begun to describe those moments when we are not awake, but with sleep disorders or simply bad sleeping habits. Sharing those moments with another dissatisfied person is not the solution.

What would happen if we embraced that other way of being human that Jesus himself inaugurated? What if amid our daily lives, we would learn to receive God's grace on a regular basis; until living according to the Spirit became our new way of being? The same Spirit that Jesus said would be like a river from within that quenches the thirst of those who trust in him.[55] On this, the evangelist John adds a truth that must have made the first recipients of his writing leap for joy: "But this He spoke concerning the Spirit, whom those believing in Him would receive; for the Holy Spirit was not yet given, because Jesus was not yet glorified".[56] So should we also jump for joy!

In an interview years ago, Dallas Willard shared that the gospel is not just about how we can be sure to go to heaven

---

[54] "30% of the young population has trouble sleeping. Sleep Unit of the Gipuzkoa Polyclinic". March 16, 2023. Accessed November 27, 2024. Https://www.policlinicagipuzkoa.com/noticias/el-30-de-la-poblacion-joven-tiene-problemas-para-dormir/

[55] "On the last and great day of the feast, Jesus stood up and lifted up his voice, saying, "If anyone is thirsty, let him come to me and drink." He who trusts in me, as the Scripture says, rivers of living water will flow from within him. This he said of the Spirit that those who trusted in him were to receive; for the Holy Spirit had not yet come, because Jesus had not yet been glorified." — John 7:37-39 NLT

[56] John 7:39 NKJV

when we die, but how to live in heaven before we die.[57] He proposed that, in its simplest form, the gospel is the fact that you can trust Jesus. Not only the ideas of Jesus, but also Jesus himself. The good news is Jesus. Not only what he can tell us, give us and do for us, but his own person. So by faith we can have access to Jesus, here and now. And it all begins with a personal invitation: "If anyone desires to come after Me, let him deny himself, and take up his cross, and follow Me"[58].

IS THERE ANOTHER WAY TO BE HUMAN?

The anxiety that characterizes the human condition and that Soren Kierkegaard calls "anguish" is what should be expected of people who have violated their own conscience. People who, trying to erase their shame, have exploited their own resources, overstepped their own boundaries, created their own survival strategies, invented their own explanations about how they got here, and struggled to believe their own lies. But despite so many efforts, the anxiety of the human condition has only gotten worse, since we do not have, in ourselves, the capacity to remedy it. All human history more than testifies to this. Every religion in the world, like everything strictly secular or non-religious (including technology, entertainment, and political, economic, educational, ideological and philosophical theories), at the end of the day are only two sides of the same coin, the insatiable and failed human effort to feel secure. In the first (religion), by trying harder to be good and

---

[57]   Dallas Willard. "Catalyst West 2010". Accessed on November 27, 2024. Https://www.youtube.com/watch?v=iwXFP1 U7f5U
[58]   Mathew 16:24 NKJV

in the second (secular or non-religious), by trying harder to be enough.

But is there another way of being human that neither religion nor non-religion knows anything about? Because it's not about trying harder to be good, nor is it about trying harder to be enough. Just look at the human record, trying harder sooner or later results in death; but if it is the Spirit who is doing it, then you can be assured it results in life and peace[59].

The Gospel is precisely about that other way of being human. Of the creation of a new humanity whose way of thinking and being does not depend on one's own effort. A way of being human that does not rely upon our flesh[60] but on the Spirit. The same Jesus who rose from the dead, can and wants to be, through His Holy Spirit, your security, your satisfaction, and your sufficiency.

Can you see it? The expression self-denial, "if anyone desires to come after Me, let him deny himself", refers to the fact that you cannot follow Jesus if you continue to strive depending on yourself. The Bible calls that, walking according to the flesh. Think about it, getting to safety has been what your whole life has been about. A life full of problems, injustices, needs, uncertainties and dangers, to which is added all the shame we try to hide. We all live on the defensive, thus exploiting ourselves, because no effort will ever be enough. To deny yourself is simply to be able to come to admit it and stop trying.

---

[59]   "… For to be minded by the flesh is death, but to be minded by the Spirit is life and peace." Romans 8:1-8
[60]   Here 'flesh' refers to our humanity.

Jesus is right, trying harder to save your own life will only lead you to lose it[61].

Following Christ necessarily requires ceasing to do what has hitherto been the most natural thing in the world for you to occupy yourself with. That is why the call to discipleship is a call to die. But what is it that dies? What is it that we are called to surrender? All our efforts to try to feel safe by being good or being enough. From there arise our screams, fights, envy, anger, jealousy, and anxiety. What else could you expect from frightened people trying to save themselves?

So, the way forward is not religion, but it is not non-religion either, it is the Gospel: Jesus doing for me what all my effort to feel safe will never achieve. In Jesus I am at last truly safe. "What I now live in my fragile humanity, I live trusting in the Son of God who loved me and gave his life for me"[62]. Because, fortunately, there's another way!

WE NEED MORE COMPREHENSIVE DISCIPLESHIP

Christian formation must take into account the damage that has been caused by living a lifetime of self-exploitation. This includes the havoc wreaked on the soul and body. Otherwise, for all practical purposes, much of what most affects the formation and deformation of our identity – including traumas, relationships, traditions, religiosity, shame, and other experiences – would remain unaddressed. An omission which would be decisively serious. People need to learn to trust Jesus for

---

[61]   Because anyone who wants to save his life will lose it... Matthew 16:25

[62]   My own paraphrase of Galatians 2:20b

their eternal destiny, but also for the here and now. Learning to die in Christ, but also to live in Christ. Sadly, we have been missing out on much of what Christ made accessible to us here and now.

We need discipleship that becomes the counterpart of Romans 12:2, where Paul exhorts us not to take on the worldly form. For even now, our society continues to instill in us its own shape, and not that of the Kingdom of God. It should also be borne in mind that the mold of the world enjoys all the resources of this century; and it feeds on the same fear that would make the first ashamed souls hide, so that no one, not even God (if such a thing were possible), could see their nakedness.

In the absence of the Gospel, we would have no choice but to succumb to the distorting influence of the world. But because of the finished work of Jesus, God gives all who receive Him and believe in Him the power to become His children,[63] and therefore to become truly human again. Based on Jesus' perfect performance credited to us, the righteous Judge of the universe can in turn call us, repentant sinners who trust His offer as one that is totally true, righteous.[64] By crediting Jesus' righteousness to us because of our faith, God declares us righteous, thus nullifying our deepest shames, and that instinctive fear of the light. Our souls no longer need to hide. Perfect love has already paid our debts in full, thus erasing them from our accounts. Our impostor becomes unnecessary,

---

[63]   John 1:12
[64]   Romans 3:26

for we are complete in Jesus and we no longer need to keep up appearances.

One of the most powerful implications of the Gospel is to finally come to know the freedom to truly be able to be ourselves. This true identity of one who is now in Christ, outside the mold of shame, knows no feeling whatsoever of being threatened. So he or she can be naked again, without being ashamed.[65] That doesn't mean you won't make mistakes again, nor that you won't need to apologize again, nor does it mean that our performance will now be flawless. What it does mean is that our nudity no longer embarrasses us. We can admit our mistakes. We can ask for forgiveness. We can laugh at ourselves. We can dispense with the affirmation of others. We can have a proper appreciation of our strengths, weaknesses, and limitations. Because we finally feel truly free and safe; "hidden with Christ, in God".[66]

If there is one thing that this society urgently needs to hear, it is everything that the Gospel teaches about identity. No topic today is as important or relevant, and the Gospel has very good news to share about it.

MAKE SURE YOUR LIGHT ISN'T DARKNESS

Jesus teaches that "No one lights a lamp and puts it under a basket"[67]. Luke's parallel text adds, "Your eye is the lamp of your body. When your eye is healthy, your whole body

---

[65]   Genesis 2:25
[66]   Colossians 3:5 NIV
[67]   Mathew 5:15 NLT

is full of light, but when it is bad, your body is full of darkness"[68].

It's urgent to make sure that the light we may think we have is not darkness. But to come to question what we had considered as light, that is; to be able to differ from ourself, we are going to require all the courage and honesty we can muster. For, to our own detriment, humility is not our default posture. It is very important to be able to distinguish light from darkness, for how much more harm will darkness itself do, if the very light with which I intend to extinguish it is also darkness. It would be like trying to put out a fire with gasoline.

Sometimes, however, it seems that the world is conspiring against us so that we do anything and everything except noticing our darkness, not to mention questioning it. Although that is precisely what we need to start doing the most.

So the next time you find yourself busy, defensive, and overthinking everything. When you again have difficulty staying quiet again or feel like you need to have the last word in every conversation. When standing still seems almost impossible or it feels hard to even breathe calmly, take a pause and ask yourself the following: What could be happening inside me that makes me act, or feel, like this? What lie could be provoking that reaction? What do I feel so deeply sure of, that I should possibly take a second look at?

Such practice has helped me spot some false identities and faulty thought patterns that tend to be very prominent in me. I'm talking about false identities that I've used to deal with my fears. Identities that include, but are not limited to, always

---

[68]   Luke 11:34 ESV

seeing me as the perfectionist, the awesome, and the expert. I also refer to fallacies such as that I must always be able to explain whatever is happening, or that I must always be aware of everything. The strong notion that I am stupid, and that I am a disgrace, and that to top it all off I am about to be discovered, is too frequent in me.

All those lies overpower me with incredible ease, especially when I'm faced with things like cognitive dissonance[69], ambiguous situations or conversations, difficult people, conflicts, new scenarios, unknown people, etc. But it's a lie that I should know everything, and it's another lie that I need to take responsibility for what someone else is responsible for, if I am to feel safe. For I will never know enough, much less always be right. My peace will never come if it depends on living up to all these lies.

Our peace can come only when the perfect judge of the universe can call us righteous. Something that is only possible by trusting in the perfect life of Jesus lived on our behalf and attributed to us. Only then, our conscience will finally stop accusing us.

Even then, the lies we have believed for years will require more than just a single illuminating event to lose their power. Whether the force of habit is messing with your muscle memory, or a trauma has begun to do the same with your cerebral amygdala; availing ourselves of our newfound freedom will need to consider that the body also remembers. As Peter Scazzero wisely points out, the body is not a minor prophet

---

[69]   Feeling uncomfortable having to deal with two contradictory beliefs.

but a major one.[70] It communicates in various ways, such as uneasiness, haste, sweaty hands, tight chest, nightmares, altered gut, agitated mind, flashbacks, and other forms of somatization. Overcoming all these symptoms and signs from our body have everything to do with learning to be human again through the power of the Gospel. There lies our hope.

MINUTES WITH THE BALL

Grounding our thinking in the Gospel then requires more than recognizing it as the truth, it will also be necessary to practice it. It's like, learning to play an instrument, or to play a sport. Theory will always be very important, but so will our sweat on the keys or on the ball.

Someone told me that the difference between elite footballers and the average player is the number of minutes they have spent since childhood touching, or kicking, the ball. And so it will also be when what one seeks to deeply internalize is the Gospel. The number of "minutes with the ball," learning and applying the gospel, will decide everything. Because the body also remembers. And whether we are talking about a piano, a ball or the truth, discipline will always be the most decisive thing. So one of the most powerful implications of that is to be able to realize that all spiritual discipline will also, necessarily, be corporeal. Because the body will never be content with being a mere spectator.

---

[70]   Peter Scazzero, The Emotionally Healthy Leader. Zondervan, Grand Rapids: Michigan, 2015, 321.

Therefore, if the body also remembers, those spiritual disciplines that help us to be more attentive to God will eventually reverse what 'practicing' our current posture, has provoked. The goal of being more mindful is at the heart of any kind of spiritual formation, whether it is Christian, secular, Muslim, agnostic or atheist. All of our habits shape us, and they will end up making us put our attention on something or someone. I want to insist on that: we are all being trained. One big difference, however, is whether we are being formed in an intentional or accidental way. The inescapable question is then, what has all of our attention?

No wonder Jesus punctuated His Sermon on the Mount with the words: "Seek first the Kingdom of God and his righteousness, and all other things will be added to you."[71] For, just as the body learned anxiety, by first seeking all the things we believed we needed, now we can also teach the body to learn the faith (and therefore to unlearn every anxious striving), seeking first the Kingdom of God and His righteousness. To "seek first" is nothing more than to focus or put all our attention on what it is we are seeking. This requires a high degree of intensity, and intentionality. Attention that nowadays seems to be diluted among the thousands of alternatives promoted by the world. It's no coincidence that the backbone of today's business model is precisely that: our attention. In many ways, the new world currency is our attention.

> "The maxim 'when things are free, the product is you' has become a fundamental axiom in the digital age. This phrase encapsulates the reality that many digital services and products that are offered for free actually

---

[71]   Matthew 6:33 NLT

monetize their users by collecting and selling their personal data, usage habits, and advertising attention. This practice has been common in social networks, search engines and free applications, where free access to the service is exchanged for a vast amount of data that companies can market with third parties or use for targeted advertising."[72]

Certainly, the pitched struggle that is taking place right now to catch our attention, even to monopolize some of the hours we spend sleeping, has no precedents. You and I are the "product" that moves this new economy. As a result, we are blurred daily between an absurd infinity of options. So, with all the sensitivity that my sense of urgency allows, I must ask you something that will define everything: what do you seek first?

---

[72]   June 11, 2024. When things are free, the product is you, but you will also pay to remain so. Article by Pure Marketing. Accessed November 27, 2024. https://www.puromarketing.com/44/213960/cuando-cosas-gratis-producto-eres-pero-ademas-pagaras-serlo. (Translation by author.)

Javier Gómez Marrero

Chapter 5

An Identity That Is Not Fragile

"The story you tell yourself about yourself is
the most important of all."

— John Ortberg
Writer, lecturer and
American Pastor

Before the beginning of Jesus' public ministry, before His first sermon, miracle, or parable, we see Jesus being baptized by John, in a spectacular beginning. The heavens opened, the Spirit of God descending upon Him, and a voice from on High with a powerful affirmation, "This is my beloved Son who brings me great joy."[73] And then, a desert. A scenario in which a decisive power encounter would take place with the very father of lies.

The desert represents our life in exile very well. That post-paradise state in which we have lost all sense of direction. The desert manages to challenge our ability to survive and therefore also brings us face to face with ourselves. Israel was in a desert for forty years; Jesus was forty days. But neither Israel nor Jesus were there alone. God was there; and someone else.

---

73   Matthew 3:17 NLT

In the wilderness, both Israel and Jesus would face their most serious temptations. In short, delicate and attractive suggestions of apparent innocence regarding the immediate course of action to pursue. There, they could see them for what they really were—demonic traps, deadly invitations attractively disguised as life and virtue, false solutions that questioned God's words. Everything fell in its proper perspective, in the desert.

But what about us? What is it that this life outside of Eden has laid bare about us to be seen by all who are willing to acknowledge it? Hidden weaknesses, double minds, doubts about our identity, a life without a magnetic north, a tendency to escape or take shortcuts, and a deep thirst that nothing can quench. Fortunately, God is also in our wilderness. But we must not forget that there is also someone else.

It is no coincidence that what Satan says to Jesus in their decisive encounter in the desert is: "If you are the Son of God...".[74] Because this struggle in exile, at the end of the day, is a struggle for one's own identity. Jesus had not finished listening to the affirmative voice of the Father calling Him the beloved Son, when the denigrating voice of His enemy was already launching the vilest attack against that very affirmation of His identity.

You and I could accuse the devil of anything but being a bad strategist. For everything in our lives depends precisely on our sense of identity. Hypothetically speaking, if he had gotten Jesus' identity to falter, even slightly, then he would have

---

[74]   Matthew 4:3 NIV

had Him right where he wanted. After all, that has always been the devil's main form of attack. And it still is.

IF YOU ARE A CHILD OF GOD

In a world where you are what you do, or what you manage to study or accumulate, or what others think or don't think of you; there is nothing more vulnerable than a sense of identity. In a society where shame is served as breakfast every day, but also as lunch and dinner, it is urgent to come to terms with who you really are. Especially in a globalized culture obsessed with putting labels on everyone. And it doesn't matter if they are good or bad labels because no one should see their identity reduced to that.

"If you are the Son of God, command that these stones become bread."[75] Few things damage the soul as much as having to prove who you are. For as we have already seen, making performance the measure of all things is a formula for disaster. A formula that has been used consistently throughout history. And the continual demand for you to turn your stones into bread, whether from people known or unknown alike, will only increase over the years. Especially in the case of those whom you serve in some capacity and those whom you call family.

The roles we share in society will define the size of the stones, their quantity, and their frequency. But you'll still have to try to transform some stones, even if they're pebbles. In the end, you will also throw a good part of that burden on your own back. Not to mention the high expectations about the

---

[75]   Matthew 4:3 NKJV

quality of the bread that everyone expects on the other side of the miracle.

To make matters worse, that same temptation will often take more than one form. Throw yourself down from the pinnacle of the temple,[76] it's just another way of intending to use your performance to define your value or measure your life, but this time through the recurring temptation to look impressive. And it is to be expected, because you have been trained by society, for a lifetime now, to take the opinion of others as a reference for your place in the world. Thus condemning you to try to meet all kinds of expectations. Which in itself is a long and heavy chain to wear. How much more so if they are unfair and unrealistic expectations. That is why the good news of the Gospel is especially relevant to everything concerning identity. For the Gospel teaches that true identity is not something we are called to produce but to receive. Your identity results from coming into existence. For this reason, human dignity is intrinsic, it does not depend on any legislation, nor on any social construct. So it is never supposed to depend on your performance.

We could then say that your true identity is a gift, both by virtue of your creation and your redemption. It is something you receive and not something you produce yourself. That is why it is permanent and never loses its luster, no matter how covered with mud it is. First you are and then you do. Understanding that would totally change the playing field. What you do does not determine who you are. It's quite the opposite! For what you are determines what you do. And since you didn't get

---

[76]   Matthew 4:5-6 NIV

here by yourself, you need whoever put you here to tell you who you are. Everyone needs to hear the Father affirm loudly and clearly what their true identity is. Something that He has done decisively in, and through, the Gospel.

THE POWER OF WORDS

When we do not hear, or accept, this decisive affirmation of the Father, then we will spend our entire lives seeking to hear it from many other people (and in their fallible words). That explains a lot of my pain, and yours. But understand this well—God has not been silent! He wants us to know who we are.

"This is my Son, whom I love; with him I am well pleased."[77] Jesus heard His Father say these words before He began His ministry and not after, for at least one very good reason. Because His identity would not result from or depend on His performance. And of course, neither does the Father's love. Those powerful words sustained Jesus far more than eating bread did. Those same words, in fact, all the words of the Father are supposed to sustain us as well. There is life, security, and true nourishment, in coming to know from the lips of the Eternal Father who we really are. But in the absence of such a statement, we will get a world like the one that surrounds us every day, where other words pretend to be able to do the work of those who were responsible for creating the cosmos. And if not, where other words seek to destroy everything that remains of that cosmos, including us.

---

[77]   Matthew 3:17 NIV

The first group of words is made up of all kinds of human effort to name and affirm us. The second group is made up of all kinds of human efforts to give us nicknames and defame us. The former do not possess what is needed to establish a permanent foundation for identity. The latter do not possess what is needed to destroy us permanently. Because neither of those two kinds of words is as powerful as God's words. That is why no degree, academic achievement, or job position should ever be confused with your name. Possibly you do this, or you studied that, but neither this nor that is you. That distinction is really important. For this very reason, every nickname, epithet or derogatory expression with which they have wanted to harm or curse you, is nullified and counteracted by what God has said about you when you are named by Him.

Recently I became a grandfather (two times in the span of a year) and I can't overstate the joy that this new season has brought to my life. But before my grandchildren (Noah and Timothy) were born, several people began asking me what I would like to name them, or if I had any suggestions to give to my children.

My answer? Simple and forceful: 'Evelyn and I had four children, and therefore, we enjoyed to satiety the beautiful privilege and the august responsibility of naming them. I have no suggestions for them. Now it's their turn at bat!

Again, none of us got here on our own. Actually, we were put here. No one can name himself except one, the One who exists in Himself and by Himself. The One who eternally named Himself as: "I Am Who I Am."[78]

---

[78]   Exodus 3:14 NIV

All creatures are named. And although many people would like to name me – and indeed they often do, in front of me and behind my back – the truth is that none of them has the right or the ability to do it well. Every human attempt to name me leaves something out, thus reducing me to something less than what I really am. Only God has both the right and the full ability to do it well.

"This is my Son, whom I love; with him I am well pleased."[79] The importance of the Gospel truth about God naming me is unparalleled. My true identity I receive exclusively from Him.

THE PLACE OF WISHES

The idea, so much in vogue today, that our desires should define us, is not new. Yet, the apparent cultural consensus on the matter is unprecedented. Most seem to assume that the mere fact of feeling a desire is sufficient justification to externalize it; and that this desire is identical to the person experiencing it, confusing desire with our identity. Such a way of thinking places us in a world where life would not only be unsustainable, but unintelligible as well.

If your desire were to end up ruling and defining you, then you would have to ask yourself: which of all those conflicting desires within you will be you? Many times you want what you hate, and other times you don't even know what you really want. This could lead you to places you would have preferred never to visit.

---

[79]   Matthew 3:17 NIV

God's words to Cain, in the midst of the deep anger that made him wish for the death of his brother Abel, are extremely relevant in this regard. Perhaps there is no passage in world literature that better describes the dynamic I intend to bring to your attention about desire.

God warns Cain: "If you do what is right, will you not be accepted? But if you do not do what is right, sin is crouching at your door; it desires to have you, but you must rule over it."[80] The imagery is about a lion lurking behind a door, of which only Cain has the power to open or to keep it closed. The reality of the existence of "sin crouching at the door" does not nullify our ability to act. In fact, it makes it much more urgent. Our control over those desires is necessary for our own safety.

Our desires certainly have their place, and God has no problem with our desires, except when our desires are in the wrong order or when they are too weak. The first happens when we make a desire the source of our identity, security, and affection, instead of a pleasure that is okay for us to enjoy in its proper place; after all, God invented pleasure! The second happens when we settle for the smallest satisfactions.

C.S. Lewis wrote the following about it:

" It would seem that Our Lord finds our desires not too strong, but too weak. We are half-hearted creatures, fooling about with drink and sex and ambition when infinite joy is offered us, like an ignorant child who wants to go on making mud pies in a slum because

---

[80]   Genesis 4:7 NIV

80

he cannot imagine what is meant by the offer of a holiday at the sea. We are far too easily pleased."[81]

So, my desires are not intrinsic to my identity, nor do they predetermine what I should do. Just because I want or can do something doesn't mean I necessarily have to do it, or that it's convenient for me to do it. This is a significant distinction that underlines the enormous importance of getting to know ourselves and our desires better. A distinction which positions us to be able to discern the difference between what I want, what I can and what I should. All of which is necessary to be able to discern between our true identity and the one that is not.

LOOKING AT OURSELVES IN FRONT OF A MIRROR

Personality tests are tools that help us gain a greater awareness of our default reactions and responses, as well as our abilities, strengths, and areas of growth. The only caveat to keep in mind is that, in my opinion, almost all these tools are actually a portrait of our false identity and not necessarily of our real one.

Put it this way, what those tests typically manage to identify are those aptitudes and strengths that we have been using as our primary survival strategies in a world that is soullessly dangerous and competitive. For in the absence of the

---

[81]   C. S. Lewis, The Weight of Glory and Other Discourses. (New York: Harper One, 2001), 26.

Gospel, we will all have to turn to none other than ourselves, with a view to trying to save our lives and those of the ones we love.

Of course it is true that much of what is innate in us is reflected in the results of those tests. So it's not that those findings are false in that regard. It's just that what always ends up taking your place in the form of a false identity is that particular way in which, out of your fears and shames, you learned to use all those descriptors to try to get what only God can give you—security, affection, and meaning. And that's precisely why all those overused features come out so obviously in your assessments. Together, these descriptors make up your main survival strategy amid our severe, and crushing, exile.

The advantage of being able to recognize what your dominant profile is, is that you can now know precisely what reactions, responses, and strategies you need to die to. Which is tremendously useful. Remember, Jesus' invitation is for you to proceed to lay hold of His perfect performance credited to you, His abundant provision and His infinite supernatural help, refusing to resort to your own performance and your limited human strength as a lifeline.

The next time you find yourself in front of a profile that was created for you by a personality assessment test, pause for a few moments and remind yourself that the portrait in front of you is not necessarily you. It's true that many of your capabilities and strengths are portrayed there, but that's not you. You can be fast, smart, good with numbers and outgoing, but that's not you. Those are some of the tools God gave you. Skills you've been overusing for a few decades now. I'm not asking you to belittle them or dismiss them. What I am inviting you to do is to discover the main way in which you are using those skills, characteristics and strengths to feel safe. You need to become familiar with the ways fear has been working as the main trigger of your personality profile. Specifically, by trying to fill your need for security, affection, and meaning by yourself.

That profile is not your core identity but your predominant "false identity". The same one you shouldn't go to for help the next time you feel inclined to do so. It is this false way of being that you need to learn to die to, or to crucify, in order to learn to receive exclusively from Jesus everything you need; instead of continuing to exploit yourself by trying to receive it from your own flesh.

Here are some well-known personality tests, or assessments:

1. The enneagram©: this system proposes nine archetypes based on the respective map of characteristics and patterns of thought, feeling and behavior. The nine archetypes are: the reformer, the helper, the achiever, the sensitive, the investigator, the loyal, the enthusiastic, the challenger, and the peacemaker.

2. Core Strengths© (Strength Deployment Inventory - SDI 2.0): This assessment, instead of focusing on what we do, helps us understand why we behave the way we do and how we relate to others. They focus on understanding the other better in order to approach them in a non-threatening way, etc.

3. Strength Finder©: This assessment measures the intensity of your talents in terms of 34 themes of the so-called Clifton Strengths, which actually represent those 34 things that people do best. They are grouped into four categories: execute

(achiever, usher, believe, consistency, intentionality, discipline, focus, responsibility, restore); to influence (activator, command, communicate, compete, maximize, self-confident, meaningful, fear); building relationships (adaptability, developer, connectivity, empathy, inclusive, harmonious, individualization, optimism, well managed), and thinking critically (analytical, context, futuristic, ideation, input, learner, intellectual, strategist).

4. Sixteen Personalities©: This appraisal measures five personality traits. Introvert versus Extrovert. Practical versus Imaginative. Logical versus Emotional. Planner versus Spontaneous. Assertive versus Self-Conscious. These five traits result in thirty-two possible combinations that are organized into sixteen profiles. These are: architect, logician, commander, innovator, lawyer, mediator, protagonist, activist, executive, ambassador, logistician, defender, entrepreneur, animator, virtuoso, and adventurer.

I could go on sharing with you about many other assessments, but I think you may already have an idea. The good news is that getting to know the ways in which you respond to problems, danger and fear, will allow you to ponder whether you want to continue reacting in that way are ready to internalize another way that has been evading you until today.

The next time you hear yourself say to yourself, "I have to_____," or you are apprehensive, overthinking everything, defensive, or busy with a lot of things; stop in your track and ask yourself, "What false identity am I wearing? Why do I feel threatened? What do I think I need, that thanks to the cross, and the love that God has already shown for me, I really no longer need? What fitness and strength of my vast carnal or human arsenal do I continually overuse to try to feel safe, but thanks to Jesus, I no longer need to use in that manner?" "I am already safe; I have already been called righteous by Him who is the righteous judge of the whole universe".

All my haste is actually shame. It's about much more than stress, and it's much more than just muscle memory. It's shame! It's a scared identity screaming at me to do something to help it hide. Something, whatever, and it needs to be quick. It could be dressing up, being impressive, looking better than I am, evading attention, or if not, seeking attention, etc., etc.

The "scream" is impossible to ignore, my muscle memory only echoes it. Only Christ manages to make that shame obsolete and He does it with His perfect performance credited in my favor. Silencing that shrill, accusing cry hidden behind all my haste. Only one thing manages to eliminate that scream. Only one thing is really necessary: Jesus! Trust Him, rest in Him, and abide in Him.

NOW WHAT?

Having come this far, what strategy will you follow to stop excusing your behavior so quickly with that classic "that's just how I am"? It's not true, you're not like that. Your false identity is like that, but you are not. So, it would help a lot to start asking yourself, what shame you are hiding behind the false identity, and what pain?

Believe me, your way out is not to try to be even more competent; for you will always fall shamefully short. Your way out is rather to deeply internalize the Gospel and embody it. Thus, start dying to that false identity that keeps swallowing every ounce of the little energy you have left, because thanks to Jesus, you can now stop hiding.

All your old habits will continue to give you a fight, despite your best efforts. Before it gets better, it will get worse. True transformation will always have to do with a series of small deaths, after which and little by little, your true "you" will emerge, the person you were really created to be.

Remember what happens between God and Jacob shortly before the blessing. God asks him, "What is your name?"[82] Why does He ask him that? That's the same question his father, Isaac, had asked a disguised Jacob posing as his brother: "Who are you, my son?"[83]

As with Jacob, God's blessing is always preceded by a long hand-to-hand struggle with Him, because making oneself vulnerable is the most difficult of our struggles, especially if it is before God. But God cannot bless us with a new name, our true name, before our difficult admission and surrender of our false identity. And so, Jacob (the cheater) finally receives the magnificent name of Israel (the prince of God).

But God's blessing involved something else: a permanent limp as a reminder of his struggle with God. In your case, if God is to bless you (and use you to bless others), He will first break you; but it is so that you may come to appreciate, and thus be able to avail yourself of, His provision of a salvation that is relevant and gloriously sufficient.

This fight is much more than symbolic. It is real and of course, it's going to hurt. God desires to strip you of your own

---

[82]   Genesis 32:27-28 NIV
[83]   Genesis 27:18

86

"Jacob". It's true, you won't be able to run as fast anymore, yet you will go much further. You will no longer need to run or hide, but now you will be a prince of God.

Like Israel, you will have discovered a deep and beautiful truth. The truth that in facing your shame and your pain that you will most intimately and deeply come to know God.

Chapter 6

A Place at the Table

"Sometimes we hear about churches that have cultures of honor, but rarely seem to be cultures where everyone is honored. The power dynamic works in such a way that honor flows uphill to the leaders... Honor seems to work much as it would in the world. The most visible receive greater glory; and the most gifted, greater attention."

— Jon Tyson
Australian Pastor and Author

The Gospel of Mark, which is the shortest of the four canonical accounts of Jesus' life, was originally addressed to a Gentile audience, that is, to people who were not Jewish. We know this because Mark devotes a good part of his limited space to explaining the particularities of the Jewish customs to which he alludes and also because, in addition to writing his work in Greek, he translated into that language every word he quotes in Aramaic.[84] So we can conclude that those accounts in which Jesus appears ministering in Gentile territory must have been of deep significance to Mark's original audience. And therefore, they should also be for us; Gentle just like them.

---

[84] As in the case of the Aramaic word — Ephphatha, which Mark translates into Greek as "be opened." (see Mark 7:34)

For example, the story of that second crowd miraculously fed by Jesus.[85]

Mark had earlier recorded that the first miraculous feeding reached more than five thousand people and that it took place in the territory of Israel. In this event, twelve baskets of leftovers were collected[86], which is equivalent to the number of tribes of Israel. However, regarding the second miraculous meal, Mark indicates that over four thousand people ate, that the disciples gathered seven baskets full, and that on that second occasion the miracle took place in the region of Decapolis[87]. Seven Gentile nations lived in that city, a number that is equivalent to the number of baskets collected.

As the old saying goes: "To someone with good understanding, a few words are enough".[88] The first twelve baskets collected, like the last seven, would seem to be shouting that there is more than enough for Israel, and that there is more than enough for the Gentiles. That superabundant universal provision would be more and more evident, throughout the entire Gospel of Mark.

A GENTILE WITHOUT AN APPOINTMENT

The story of the Syro-Phoenician woman, and of her demon-possessed daughter, is on point. Her arrival on stage must have felt more like an undesirable interruption. The text reads as follows:

---

85   Mark 8:1-10
86   Mark 6:43
87   Mark 7:31
88   Or "a word to the wise, is sufficient."

" And from thence he arose, and went into the borders of Tyre and Sidon, and entered a house, and would have no man know it: but he could not be hidden. For a certain woman, whose young daughter had an unclean spirit, heard of him, and came and fell at his feet: the woman was a Greek, a Syrophenician by nation; and she besought him that he would cast forth the devil out of her daughter. But Jesus said unto her, Let the children first be filled: for it is not right to take the children's bread, and to cast it unto the dogs. And she answered and said unto him, yes, Lord: yet the dogs under the table eat of the children's crumbs. And he said unto her, for this saying go thy way; the devil is gone out of thy daughter. And when she had come to her house, she found the devil gone out, and her daughter laid upon the bed. And again, departing from the coasts of Tyre and Sidon, he came unto the sea of Galilee, through the midst of the coasts of Decapolis. And they bring unto him one that was deaf and had an impediment in his speech; and they beseech him to put his hand upon him. And he took him aside from the multitude, and put his fingers into his ears, and he spit, and touched his tongue; and looking up to heaven, he sighed, and saith unto him, Ephphatha, that is, Be opened. And straightway his ears were opened, and the string of his tongue was loosed, and he spoke plain. And he charged them that they should tell no man: but the more he charged them, so much the more a great deal they published it; and were beyond measure astonished, saying, He hath done all things well: he maketh both the deaf to hear, and the dumb to speak".[89]

---

[89]   Mark 7:24-37

Mark says that Jesus himself tried to go unnoticed in those parts. So the chances that troubled woman had of accessing the help she so desperately needed were minimal. And Jesus' words at her request only seem to confirm what He said; since He immediately tells her: "It's not right"[90].

I think that the key to understanding one of the strangest ways of proceeding in the life of Jesus is precisely in the phrase "It's not right." Because the obligatory question would be, It isn't okay for whom? Sometimes one learns that what is not right for oneself is perfectly right for God. Sometimes we also feel very confident that we are seeing things exactly as God sees them, but He comes to our attention by correcting us on the spot. This invites us to reconsider how aligned our thinking really is with those nineteen baskets of His superabundant universal provision.

The woman's brilliant response highlights a significant fact in the Gospel of Mark. Information that might otherwise go unnoticed. James Edwards comments that "this woman is the first person in Mark who understands a parable of Jesus... the fact that the woman can answer Jesus using his same parable shows that she has come to understand its true meaning."[91]

Seeing it in this way, one would have to conclude that this woman surpasses even Jesus' own students. Time and again those privileged disciples of Jesus seemed to be still light years away from understanding their beloved master. Sadly, they don't even realize that. What's more, they can't seem to

---

[90]   Mark 7:27
[91]   James R. Edwards, The Gospel according to Mark (The Pillar New Testament Commentary). (Grand Rapids: Eerdmans, 2002), 221.

even begin to entertain the possibility that they are misunder-
standing Jesus. That is why they had been quick to try to tell
Jesus what He Himself should do with that annoying woman:
"Send her away, for she keeps crying out after us."[92] Isn't that
same thing happening to us, His current students, as well?

That woman does nothing more than listen to Jesus'
parable, when not only does she already understand it, but she
finds in it the very answer she needs to receive help. As if to
say, "It isn't okay to eat the bread, but how about eating the
crumbs?" And Jesus, evidently moved, would end up giving
her a standing ovation. Jesus basically says to her: "Woman,
you just hit a home run; good answer woman!" So good is the
response of this woman, that she not only manages to extract
tremendous applause from Jesus but also a tremendous miracle. Why? Well, because she has just underlined a truth that
deserves all our attention. And by that I mean the crumbs that
fall from the table.

This is an early manifestation of God's mercy toward
the Gentile people. The same abundant provision of mercy
that was supposedly not right. It is explained in the Gospel of
Mark with the surprising outcome of a highly improbable encounter between Jesus and a Gentile woman, to whom the
Gospel dawns. A Syrophoenician woman whose name we
don't even know. Someone who, according to the supposed
experts and students of Jesus, was the least qualified person to
do so. A woman, who to top it off, was not even Jewish.

God thinks very differently from us. You and I see so
little! You and I hear so poorly! And as if that were not enough,

we judge much worse. But follow me, as there is still much more to this woman's fascinating story of abundance.

THIS IS NOT A TEST!

Jesus is not testing this woman. Something that has sometimes been suggested when trying to explain a passage, where at first glance, Jesus does not seem to act like Jesus. This is not a test. This is the Gospel breaking paradigms and prejudices. This is new wine, which will always demand new wineskins if the wine is to be used.[93] This is the "no one puts a new patch on old clothes"[94], if it is to be used again. This is the "you have heard that it was said... but I tell you."[95]

Breaking all these old paradigms will always be very uphill. Even God Himself will again and again draw on His great creativity to help us see what we often find so difficult to see because of the hardness of our hearts. Sometimes God uses a crisis, other times God uses our losses, and if not, our own season of life. Events that come to us loaded with changes, whether they are mild or dramatic.

I suspect that is precisely why the crumbs of God appear here. Crumbs with which God, in consortium with this brilliant woman, will break down millenary prejudices based on erroneous concepts about the genuine appearance, and the typical behavior, of God. Many of which, sadly, are still alive and kicking.

---

93   Luke 5:37-39
94   Matthew 9:16a
95   Matthew 5:43-44

Therefore, a crumb of God's superabundant universal provision will always be more than enough. For, like the little grain of mustard seed once sown[96], or like the little leaven that a woman mixes into three measures of flour[97], the Kingdom of God—even if it goes unnoticed at first and advances slowly— is an unstoppable force! And it is precisely this reality that pushes and encourages a woman to challenge, even if gently, a Jewish convention of the time that urgently needed to be. Hence she dares to say to Jesus: "What I ask for is only like a crumb of bread." She doesn't respond with, "How dare you speak to me like that, Jesus?" But she is not resigned either. Something that, sadly, I have done too many times in my life. What she basically says to Jesus is, "I don't ask you for this as if I could earn it by being good nor enough, I ask you because you are good, and more than enough!" And on the grand stage of what Jesus would eventually end up doing for all of us, casting out that demon would be just a crumb of bread. That's how powerful this Jesus is.

This woman truly understood. She understood even better than we do almost two thousand years later. Here we read prejudice and insensitivity, and we even read an unfriendly Jesus. But she only sees the superabundance of Grace that is available to all of us. So she manages to understand that what she is asking of Jesus is only a crumb.

That says a lot about the character and immeasurable power of this everlasting Gospel. For however wonderful that

---

96   Matthew 13:31-32
97   Mathew 13:33-37

crumb of bread was to that woman, whoever trusts in the merits of Christ and not in any merit of their own, obtains much more. To put it in terms of the parable, the bread of the children. And we urgently need to come to appreciate that the children's bread is more valuable than any miracle, much more valuable. Absolute forgiveness of all your sins. Broad access to the very presence of God. Partaking in a new spiritual nature. Having the Spirit of God dwelling in us leading us into all truth. The beautiful communion of the saints. To be seated with Christ in the Heavenly places, above all principality, and power, and might, and dominion[98], now and forever. Healing from all the trauma and anxiety that has characterized us. A significant role in God's mission and His help in it. Talking to God! If all that were not enough, the glory that will be manifested in us later. That's the real bread; the rest is crumbs.

In the words of the psalmist, "You prepare a table before me in the presence of my enemies."[99] David is saying, "God is so powerful and good that He prepares a feast for me of bountiful delicacies under the helpless gaze of my enemies. My peace does not depend on the presence or absence of enemies, but on the presence of God and the superabundant provision of goodness for my life that always accompanies Him."

Too often we fail to see the feast of God that David saw; and as a result, we die of hunger and of chronic worries and anxieties. All because we do not see or taste, as we are able to do, the extraordinary delicacy of God. Sadly, we spend our time consuming the abundant content served to us by digital

---

[98]   Ephesians 1:19-21
[99]   Psalms 23:5 NIV

96

media algorithms. Because of this, we are still filled with fears, guilt, anger, misunderstandings, traumas, and what is worse— severely distracted while all the time hiding behind the old fig leaves that our parents used[100].

What's your fig leaf? Perfectionism, do you not accept making mistakes? Surrender your leaf and rest. You don't need to be perfect, Jesus is already perfect for you. Is it control, do you try to control the outcomes to feel safe? Surrender your leaf and rest, Jesus is in charge now. Look first for the public policies of the Kingdom of God, and let God take care of the outcomes. Maybe it's pleasing everyone, are you trying to earn the love of others? Surrender your fig leaf and rest, you are accepted thanks to the merits of the Son of God. You have been included. You really belong!

LOVE IN A THOUSAND LANGUAGES

A second account is on point regarding the universal superabundance contained in the Gospel of Mark. An account about the impressive healing of a deaf-mute man.

Mark writes —

"Then Jesus left the vicinity of Tyre and went through Sidon, down to the Sea of Galilee and into the region of the Decapolis. There some people brought to him a man who was deaf and could hardly talk, and they begged Jesus to place his hand on him. After he took him aside, away from the crowd, Jesus put his fingers into the man's ears. Then he spit and touched the man's tongue. He looked up to heaven and with a deep sigh said to him, "Ephphatha!" (which means

---

[100]   Genesis 3:7

"Be opened!"). At this, the man's ears were opened, his tongue was loosened, and he began to speak plainly. Jesus commanded them not to tell anyone. But the more he did so, the more they kept talking about it. People were overwhelmed with amazement. "He has done everything well," they said. "He even makes the deaf hear and the mute speak"[101].

What first catches my attention is not so much the impressive healing that the man would immediately receive, but the strange gestures of Jesus, moments before healing him. What's all this stuff about sticking your fingers in your ears, smearing saliva on your fingers, and touching the tongue of the mute?

I remind you that, in order to understand an ancient text, we will always face the enormous difficulty of bridging the distance between the text and us. There is cultural distance, but there is also historical distance. There is linguistic distance that includes, for example, the figures of language, among many other important variables that are taken into account in human communication. Then there is the religious distance; and add to that the significant scientific distance. Well, to all that we should also add a distance that almost none of us are very used to considering. I am referring to the sensitive distance of the omnipresent functional diversity.

The world is not seen in the same way, nor is it interpreted in the same way, from the perspective of a person with functional diversity. The perspectives of the blind person, and the paraplegic person, and those on the autism spectrum, to

---

[101]   Mark 7:31-37 NIV

name just a few, will necessarily be different. The same happens with the perspective of the deaf-mute person. That is why we could easily overlook much of what is taking place in this precious passage. We will not understand, until we manage to enter, even partially, into the daily reality of that deaf-mute.

What is Jesus doing here? Timothy Keller says that, "Those gestures are not a hocus-pocus or anything like that. It is, rather, sign language."[102] Jesus sought to enter the silent world of that man in the full sense of that phrase. And that's nothing short of beautiful. Jesus was practically saying to him, "I'm going to help you." What would be his surprise, to discover, that Jesus also spoke his language. The silence of those gestures, between Jesus and the deaf-mute, is certainly deafening to me. Only Jesus! No wonder those people exclaim: "He has done everything well!"[103].

What is the Gospel? Knowing that there is a place for us at the table. But also for those who would be left off the table by many of our old prejudices. That is why God continues to allow all these "inconvenient interruptions". Sometimes allowing a pandemic, a hurricane, an executive order, or a decision to go wrong. In the alternative, he may allow a prodigal son, or a business that doesn't take off, or a conflict, or a failed vacation. Other times allowing for a layoff, a broken relationship, a crisis, or a deep disappointment. Situations that will often challenge our prejudices and assumptions.

Taking advantage of your new wine will always require new wineskins. Changes that look tremendously intimidating,

102   Timothy Keller, King's Cross: The Story of The World in The Life of Jesus. (Dutton Press, 2011), 93.
103   Mark 7:37 NIV

with humiliating learning curves. Inconvenient interruptions through which God continues to call us to that new thing that He Himself is allowing and sometimes even presiding over. Often adding that awkward, but necessary, "you heard that it was said... but I tell you."[104]

That's what being a true disciple is all about. To be a disciple is to be an apprentice who is continually corrected and encouraged. To be a disciple is to stumble over elaborate learning curves. To learn something is to hear ourselves say, "I always believed this, and I only now discovered that it is not so." To be a student is to learn with Jesus how the world works and how we ourselves are supposed to work.

Equity and justice are values of the Kingdom of God. Too much damage has already been perpetrated against people created in the image of God. Sadly, some of that damage has also been brought about by people supposedly acting in His Name, but representing Him in a terribly wrong way. They have, in the process, alienated many whom God really desires to draw closer to Himself.

As a pastor, I want to be part of the solution to our grave social ills and to resolutely combat the destructive lies that spread them. Certainly, we should begin by admitting our own sins as a society and humbly asking forgiveness from every person who has been victimized, either by our action or inaction. The first step in the transformation of any situation is the admission of what is wrong, followed by a profound change of attitude and behavior with respect to what is wrong. I will always be the first to be grateful and celebrate the enormous and

---

[104]   Matthew 5:43-44

ongoing transformation brought about in my own life by the undeserved forgiveness of my countless and embarrassing sins.

I also understand that another important step would be to produce solutions that embody the very inclusivity we stand for. Regarding the real possibility of such a consensus, I would like to emphasize that, in the most famous prayer of all, the Lord's Prayer, many of us ask for God's Kingdom to come. Prayer with which we are asking, among many other things, that justice and purity be the norm in all our relationships.

Imagine what that would mean for all economic, employment, social, and family transactions in our respective countries. We also ask that the day come when international relations will be generous and dignified, and that all contempt and mistreatment against our neighbors will disappear, as well as that which has been committed against children, young people, the elderly, women, the most vulnerable, other ethnic groups and nature itself, including animals.

In part it could be said that the Kingdom of God is how the world would be and look if God ran the show[105]. And while we will not all necessarily agree as to how we can come to shape a more just world, and even as to exactly what that world might look like, let us at least grant that we agree more than we might have assumed about how desirable a more just world is.

For my part, I want to do everything I can to create the conditions so that more people have a genuine opportunity to choose to live in such a world. That is why I will continue to

---

[105]   I once heard that expression from a sermon by NT Wright, but I haven't been able to identify the whole reference so that I might provide it.

preach the Gospel, but I will also (and precisely because of the Gospel) defend the right of those who do not think exactly like me to differ from me.

What if more of us could respectfully invite the others to tell us their story, seeking to better understand their respective predicaments? What if others could also hear, in the same spirit, our own experience with the love and power of the God of the Gospel? The One who can redeem all our sufferings, always keeping our best interest in mind. The One who can do in, by and through us, what we would never achieve left to our own devices. By His Grace, we have not been left at the mercy of ourselves, which is very good news.

There's a place for us at God's table, and for all those who want to come. Jesus' invitation remains just as inclusive, and just as instructive. "If anyone desires to come after Me, let him deny himself, and take up his cross, and follow Me"[106].

Jesus speaks our language. He does everything right, even if sometimes, it may not feel that way to us.

---

[106]   Matthew 16:24

Chapter 7

A Good Life

"Our careers, our goods, our natural and spiritual gifts, our health, are they our possessions or do we simply manage them in the name of the One who gave them? Compulsive people consider them their own; the people called by God don't. If compulsive people lose them, they suffer major crises. If people called by God lose them, nothing substantial changes. Their private world remains the same, perhaps even stronger."

— Gordon MacDonald
American pastor and author

Have you ever stopped to think about the questions God asks?

To Adam: "Where are you?"[107]

To Cain: "Where is your brother?"[108]

To Jacob: "What is your name?"[109]

To the blind man: "What do you want me to do for you?"[110]

The lame in the pool of Bethesda: "Do you want to be healed?"[111]

---

[107]   Genesis 3:9
[108]   Genesis 4:9
[109]   Genesis 32:27
[110]   Mark 10:51
[111]   John 5:6

To the slave girl Hagar in the desert: "Where do you come from, where are you going?"[112]

To the Samaritan woman at the well: "Can you give me some water?"[113]

To Peter: "Do you love me... Do you love me... Do you love me?"[114]

God wants to work with the substance, the real matter, of our actions. He is always after our spacious and elusive inner world. Authentic motivations, veiled assumptions, fears, traumas, desires, and dreams. God is especially interested in our countless blind spots. Those realities that you and I don't even know that we don't know.

That is why we are not surprised by Jesus' famous conversation with a young man who, believing himself to be very sure of his own question, ended up learning that he does not know what he is asking or who he is asking. An interesting exchange that is recorded in the first of the four Gospels. Matthew writes:

> "Now behold, one came and said to Him, "Good Teacher, what good thing shall I do that I may have eternal life?" So, He said to him, "Why do you call Me good? No one is good but One, that is, God. But if you want to enter life, keep the commandments." He said to Him, "Which ones?" Jesus said, "'You shall not murder,' 'You shall not commit adultery,' 'You shall not steal,' 'You shall not bear false witness,' 'Honor your father and your mother,' and 'You shall love your neighbor as yourself.'" The young man said to Him, "All these things I have kept from my youth. What do

---

112   Genesis 16:8
113   John 4:7
114   John 21:15-19

I still lack?" Jesus said to him, "If you want to be perfect, go, sell what you have and give to the poor, and
you will have treasure in heaven; and come, follow
Me." But when the young man heard that saying, he
went away sorrowful, for he had great possessions.
Then Jesus said to His disciples, "Assuredly, I say to
you that it is hard for a rich man to enter the kingdom
of heaven. And again, I say to you, it is easier for a
camel to go through the eye of a needle than for a rich
man to enter the kingdom of God." When His disciples heard it, they were greatly astonished, saying,
"Who then can be saved?" But Jesus looked at them
and said to them, "With men this is impossible, but
with God all things are possible." Then Peter answered
and said to Him, "See, we have left all and followed
You. Therefore, what shall we have?" So, Jesus said to
them, "Assuredly I say to you, that in the regeneration,
when the Son of Man sits on the throne of His glory,
you who have followed Me will also sit on twelve
thrones, judging the twelve tribes of Israel. And everyone who has left houses or brothers or sisters or father
or mother or wife or children or lands, for My name's
sake, shall receive a hundredfold, and inherit eternal
life. But many who are first will be last, and the last
first"[115].

WHY DO YOU CALL ME GOOD?

Pastor Carmelo Terranova, who was a native of Argen-
tina and served for many years in my native Puerto Rico, was
an important influence in my life and ministry. For many years
he pastored his beloved local congregation at Catedral de La

[115]   Matthew 19:16-30 NKJV

Esperanza Church and many of us who, even from a distance, were able to see him as a pastor and mentor.

In my examination for ministerial candidacy with The Alliance, Terranova actively participated as a member of the Council on Ordination and Credentials. I still remember when looking at me he said, "Javier, you're not a pastor yet." And he immediately proceeded to remind me that the international evangelist Luis Palau himself, on occasion of an interview in which someone called him a "pro of the Gospel", quickly replied: "A pawn you mean? No one becomes an expert in something as profound as the Gospel."

Terranova was well known in Puerto Rico for his gifts as a preacher, God used him powerfully. But he was also well known among us for what he himself came to call as "terranovadas", phrases or reactions that, due to being unexpected and poignant, made some feel a little uncomfortable. Of course, most of the time, they would do us great good, although at the time almost no one would felt that way. Terranova mastered the border between the politically incorrect and the surprisingly brilliant. In addition, he used to go off the "unspoken script" that many expect to be followed rigorously. How much it blessed me that he went off script from time to time! His famous way of stunning people with some eloquent occurrence made some evade him or as we say on the island, "get out of his way"; although many others, like me, what we sought from him was an appointment to look for good counsel.

I think Jesus also made good use of his own "terranovadas" and often went off script. The passage of the rich young ruler was one of those occasions; and specifically I am referring

106

to Jesus' response to the young man's greeting: "Why do you call me good?"[116]

I don't think Jesus was conceding for a moment that he himself wasn't good or that it was somehow wrong to call him good. He just wanted to help the young man hear his own greeting a little better. Because starting with that greeting, soon all his other assumptions would be turned upside down. How much good it does us when Jesus acts in the same way with our own assumptions, while giving us that same look of love[117].

Immediately after, Jesus says to him, "You know the commandments..."[118]. What was Jesus aiming for when he decided to direct the conversation towards the Ten Commandments? I am convinced that he was at least looking for those commandments to do their thing. For it is one thing to know the Ten Commandments, and another to have those commandments know you. It's one thing to read the Bible, and it's another for the Bible to read you. Judging the Law is one thing, but for the Law to judge you is another thing entirely. Because then, the young man's request would have been different. Instead of asking, "What should I do?"[119], he would have begged him: "Help me, please Jesus, help me!".

Sadly, many people confuse the gospel with "What else do I need to do?" For this reason, some reject it as too difficult, as something they want nothing to do with. Others end up practicing some "try harder Christianity" of a sort. Without really changing and without genuine freedom, they always end

116   Mark 10:18
107   "Then Jesus looked upon him and loved him." — Mark 10:21
118   Luke 18:20
119   Mark 10:17

up lacking something, alone, inadequate, hidden, but above all tired and bitter.

John Ortberg Wrote:

"Let's call him Hank! Hank has been going to church since he was a child and is now in his 70s. Everyone knows him, but in reality no one knows him. His wife can't stand him and his children barely feel free enough to talk to him. He cares neither for the poor nor for foreigners, and he does not care for all those who do not belong to the church. The last straw is that Hank very harshly judges all those who do attend his church. One day, an elder in the church asked him, "Hank, are you happy?" Without blinking and still frowning, he replied, "Yes." "Well," said the old man, "then tell your face." Hank's outward appearance reflected a tragic reality: Every week Hank attended his church, without it making a dent in him. And here's the most inexplicable thing of all: no one in the church seemed to be surprised. No one called an emergency meeting of any committee to examine this strange case of a person who was not changing in spite of so many sermons. No one was expecting Hank to change, so no one was surprised that it wasn't happening. There was a different kind of expectation in the church: many expected Hank not to miss a service, and of course to read his Bible, give money, and serve in some ministry. But no one was really expecting that over the months, years, and a few decades, Hank would become more loving and joyful. So no one was shocked that it didn't happen."[120]

Similarly, Dallas Willard wrote:

---

[120]   John Ortberg, The Life You've Always Wanted: Spiritual Disciplines for Ordinary People. (Zondervan, Grand Rapids: Michigan, 2009), 28.

"How many people are radically and permanently distanced from the Way because of insensitive, bitter, unjust and pedantic Christians? Sadly, Christians like that are everywhere... Spirituality incorrectly and cultivated is a major source of human misery and rebellion against God."[121]

Obviously, it is not supposed to be so.

Jesus' band of disciples, from the very beginning, had those who would pass for disciples, without really being so. Jesus said that they would look like the branch of a vine that bears no fruit. Judas, who was eventually to be cut off from among them, is the classic example. On the surface, Judas seemed connected to Jesus, but there was nothing about him to suggest true life!

Once again, the Gospel always produces dramatic evidence of authentic life in the one who embraces it. It is not in vain that the Bible calls it salvation! Also, new life! On another occasion he calls it a new creation. It is impossible to embrace the Gospel and not begin to experience life that is life to the full. Impossible! Listening to and understanding the words of Jesus will always do its thing in us; it is cause and effect. Something that many, sadly, neither know nor experience, even though they have supposedly heard those same words. It is because, in honor of the truth, for one reason or another, they do not have embraced the gospel and therefore, the implications of the Gospel have not yet dawned on them. Jesus puts it this way: " Jesus said to them, "This is the only work God wants

---

[121]   John Ortberg, Laurie Pederson, Judson Poling, Fully Devoted: Living Each Day in Jesus' Name. (Zondervan, Grand Rapids: Michigan, 2009), 16.

from you: Believe in the One He has sent"[122]. One can spend one's life among believers and still not embrace, let alone understand, the glorious meaning of these wonderful words.

The analogy of the true vine and its fruitful branches,[123] does not intend to contrast people connected to Christ who bear fruit with those supposedly connected to Christ who do not. As if that were even possible, to be genuinely connected to Christ and not bear fruit. Rather, this powerful analogy contrasts what it is to be authentically alive with the mere appearance of life. Attributing all the difference exclusively to the fact of being connected to Christ, thus underscoring the powerful effect that the Gospel will have on all who embrace it.

Therefore, John writes, "But these are written that you may believe that Jesus is the Messiah, the Son of God, and that by believing you may have life in his name."[124] The branch with fruit speaks precisely of that life. The life that you and I cannot produce by ourselves or in a million years no matter how hard we try. That's the point. Jesus does not try to intimidate us so that we step up, take responsibility and begin to produce. The fruitful life requires more than mere willpower or that famous "do your part". At the end of the day it's not that you don't want to, it's that you can't, by yourself, live that life, no matter how much you want it.

Jesus did not come merely to help us become better; He came to impart His very life to us. To do for you, in you, and through you, what neither you, nor I, nor anyone else can do. He came, not only to give you heaven one day, but also

---

[122]   John 6:29 NIV
[123]   John 15:5
[124]   John 20:31

that life of peace, joy, patience, kindness, faithfulness, self-control, and love that we all long for, but that seems to elude us all.

This is the truth, you can achieve many things if you try hard enough. The young man was rich! But one cannot see, much less experience, that life that is truly good, without trusting God. That is the reason why that rich young ruler goes to Jesus, because having fulfilled everything he believed was expected of him to enter the Kingdom, he did not yet feel the life of the Kingdom within him. Jesus' own disciples, at that point, would agree that the young having done all that, should indeed already be feeling that abundant life. Still, it was not like that. I am afraid that even today and in our churches, like that young man, many continue to wonder: "Why don't I feel that abundant life?".

WHAT DO YOU WANT MOST?

"Do you want to be perfect?"[125] Do you want to be well, and not just look well? Do you want to be complete? Well, then, "... Go, sell everything you have and give to the poor, and you will have treasure in heaven. Then come, follow me"[126].

This must have turned the young man's other assumptions upside down. To do what Jesus was asking of him would show that a significant new inner reality had taken place in him. That inner reality would be the Kingdom of God. The peace that comes from the certainty of knowing that we are loved,

---

125   Matthew 19:21a NIV
126   Mark 10:21 NIV

forgiven, protected, justified, and complete in Jesus. For then the Kingdom of God would have entered into him; and he, in turn, would have effectively entered the Kingdom of God. But on the contrary, refusing to obey Jesus could only mean one thing: that insecurity and anxiety still reigned within him. And how could he not hold on to his money then?

The Kingdom of God does not suffer from anxiety or sleep disorders. Nor is it afraid that tomorrow it will lack something. So the truest evidence that the Kingdom is already living in you is not what we might suppose—religious rigor—but the soul resting safely and fully satisfied in the One who deserves our full confidence.

That is what God calls love: to help a rich young man understand that the fear that reigns in his soul is totally alien to the life of the Kingdom that he claims to know. Inviting him to enjoy the profound peace of those who no longer need to flee from God nor from themselves. To learn to be truly human is to begin to live in that Kingdom now, and for that same Kingdom to begin to live in you as well.

THE GOSPEL IS REST

Relying upon your ability to generate money, your reputation, or whatever you manage to excel in, is not enough, nor is it sustainable. No wonder you're so tired. Therefore, "come to me, all you who labor and are heavy laden, and I will give you rest"[127], is music to my ears. It is the most important invitation we have ever received. We are invited to rest from trying

---

[127]   Matthew 11:28

to quiet our guilt and fear by using our accomplishments, strengths, contacts, money, beauty, influence, and the like. So that having been credited with the perfect performance of Jesus in substitution for our sins, then our shames and fears are eradicated. For Jesus is enough. That is why Jesus' question to the young man: "Why do you call me good?" is key. Because our only chance of peace lies in coming to believe that He is good.

WHAT IS THE GOOD LIFE?

" Verily I say unto you, that a rich man shall hardly enter into the Kingdom of Heaven"[128]. The culture of those days assumed that being rich was a sign of God's approval. The good life consisted of getting rich. Exactly the same as today. To flourish is to travel a lot, to eat wherever we want, to associate with those who move the world, to dress well, to look impressive, etc. But far from conceding that premise, Jesus rather confronts it, beginning with his own disciples (and specifically Peter). Jesus basically says to him, in our words, something like, "Listen to me, Peter, you're right about one thing, but you're wrong about the other. It's true, the life everyone is looking for is humanly impossible. On the other hand, that rich young ruler is no better off than you."

Think about it, according to Jesus, those whom this century considers to be first, the next century considers to be

---

[128]   Matthew 19:23

last.[129] In His Kingdom, life flourishes not by turning to one-self to save it, but by denying oneself to receive it. And what would it be like otherwise? Nothing dehumanizes us as much as what we must pay to be first in the eyes of this world. And nothing humanizes us more than to be able to see in our own lives that what is impossible for man is possible for God. Jesus then presents us with a very different picture of what authentic flourishing is. "Truly I tell you…no one who has left home or brothers or sisters or mother or father or children or fields for me and the gospel will fail to receive a hundred times as much in this present age: homes, brothers, sisters, mothers, children and fields—along with persecutions—and in the age to come eternal life"[130]. That factor of a hundred times more is used to refer to a better life, the true good life. The good life that many look for by living according to the way of this age, is surpassed a hundredfold by the life made available by living in the way of the Kingdom of God.

EVERYTHING IS UPSIDE DOWN

The constant media bombardment to which you and I are subjected daily can be summed up in one word: worry. Worry about tomorrow. Worry about the upcoming elections. Worry about what that other person said, or didn't say. Worry about artificial intelligence and its lethal possibilities. It goes on, and on. But Jesus teaches us to do the exact opposite. " Therefore do not worry about tomorrow, for tomorrow will

---

[129]   Mark 10:31
[130]   Mark 10:29-30 NIV

worry about itself. Each day has enough trouble of its own"[131]. According to Jesus, learning to be truly human includes learning to live only one day at a time.

In the eyes of this age, Jesus' next statement doesn't make much sense either: "Blessed are the meek because they will inherit the earth"[132]. If you ask anyone on the street who will inherit the earth, most people will answer something like, "The ones with the largest army." How could anyone today get to own land by turning the other cheek? Or by blessing the one who curses him; or by loving the enemy, or by suffering reproach? But, once again I stop and hear Jesus' clarification to Peter, something like: "It's not true, Peter, that rich young ruler is no better off than you. And although he seems to have it all, he is deeply dissatisfied, anxious, and empty. His impressive success has not been enough and cannot be. That's why he's here, asking me all these questions".

Jesus sees in that rich young man true poverty. Everyone else envies him. Jesus pities him. In the end, gaining the whole world is not only good for the soul, its deadly.[133] The good life has nothing to do with an exhausted and labored soul, but it does have everything to do with a soul that is satisfied and comforted, one that is being directed and protected by the One who is infinitely competent to do so. The One who continues to call us to Himself with the tenderest, and to the point, of invitations: "Come, follow me! …".[134]

---

131   Matthew 6:34 NIV
132   Matthew 5:5 NIV
133   "For what will it profit a man, if he gains the whole world, and loses his soul? Or what reward will a man give for his soul?" — Matthew 16:26
134   Matthew 4:19 NIV

Javier Gómez Marrero

Chapter 8

A Soul That is Not Divided

"Anger is the divine reaction to sin. Atonement is necessary because human beings are under the wrath and judgment of God. Unless we give real content to the wrath of God, unless we hold that men really deserve to be punished by God with the painful consequences of their evil actions, we empty God's forgiveness of its meaning."

— George Eldon Ladd
Renowned minister, Canadian
professor and theologian

We need to admit to ourselves that having been driven out of Paradise and into exile has traumatized us. So, in addition to being forgiven, we need to be healed of deep anguish and shame.

It doesn't matter how much we pretend that life is going well, the trauma of sin haunts and torments us. Dr. Bessel van Der Kolk, an expert in what has come to be known as "post-traumatic stress disorder"[135] puts it like this: the body keeps the score.[136]

---

[135]   Post-traumatic stress disorder is amental health illness triggered by a frightening situation, whether you've experienced or witnessed it. Symptoms can include flashbacks, nightmares, and severe distress, as well as uncontrollable thoughts about the situation.
[136]   That's the title of his landmark book: The Body Keeps the Score.

Today we know that any terrifying event from which the affected person does not manage to recover well, or that lacks some definitive resolution or "closure" that restores well-being and full functionality, qualifies as traumatic. And it's important to understand that our bodies internalize both the traumatic event itself and the instinctive survival response activated by it. Survival response that will continue to be activated, even long after the traumatic event; particularly by those triggers that bring the trauma to memory, making us relive it over and over again. Thus denying victims the possibility of continuing with their lives, freezing them in time. Any survival response that fails to materialize adequately in a timely manner will take the form of an endless spiral seeking resolution or healing. Years after the traumatic event, it will continue to wreak havoc on the victim's daily life. Nothing meets all aspects of description of such a traumatic event better than sin itself. And believe me, our bodies are keeping that score too.

THE PAST HAUNTS US

In addition, in order to live with ourselves we will need to convince ourselves that we are incapable of doing anything shameful. So in this precise act of denial, we will be left without reasons or categories at hand to be able to adequately explain our experience of evil. So, since we can't 'be okay', then we can only try to 'look' ok. And that's why we all run away from the light. A reality that will inevitably result in a divided soul. Expression with which I refer to the disintegration or lack of integrity between our inner and outer life, in other words, a double life.

That is why confession becomes an indispensable practice for those who aspire to be fully healthy. For by matching what happens inside us with what happens on the outside, the soul finally becomes one piece again, coherent, in harmony with reality, instead of operating from the incoherence of lies that futilely try to our conscience. But shortly after confessing, we are able to think with true clarity again. Interestingly then, the more we confess our sins, the more whole we are. It is true that it will cost us a lot—too much for the way of thinking of this world—but only then will we begin to heal. Only then will we finally be truly well.

Dr. Juliet Font[137] led a study the results of which seemed to suggest that among the companies researched, certain companies that made the most mistakes were the most successful. A result that, at first, didn't make sense to her. How did those other companies with fewer errors, and therefore presumably better managed, fall behind economically? She decided to investigate further and found that it wasn't that those who reported making more mistakes, in fact made more mistakes; it was rather that they confessed making more mistakes than the others. Those that reported making fewer mistakes, actually made many more, but had decided to hide them. In other words, those companies were lying! But, although they could alter the data, they could not alter the painful consequences of

---

[137]   Juliet Font explaining the results of her doctoral thesis that finally gave rise to her book A Minute to Think. CNLP 446 | Juliet Font on Productivity Thieves, the Hidden Cost of Busyness, How to Add White Space to Your Work and Life. Accessed: November 27, 2024. Https://careynieuwhof.libsyn.com/cnlp-446-juliet-funt-on-productivity-thieves-the-hidden-cost-of-busyness-how-to-add-white-space-to-your-work-and-life

those unconfessed errors, because sooner or later they ended up failing. Likewise, we will never experience meaningful healing until we begin to recognize the "plank in your eye"[138] and to confess it in front of others. We need to be in the light with others, admitting to others the truth about ourselves. Ironically, to our own detriment, Christian families and churches seem to be the last place where this happens. We settle for pretending that we are a community, evading the hard work of truly becoming one.[139] We only agree to ignore all disagreements, hiding them under a rug that has long since become too small to cover them all.

Richard Foster, author of the classic The Celebration of Christian Spiritual Disciplines, wrote:

> "Confession is a very difficult spiritual practice for us because we see the congregation of believers as a sharing among saints and not as a sharing among sinners. We come to feel that everyone has advanced so far toward holiness that we feel isolated and alone in our sin. We imagine that we are the only ones who have not yet crossed the avenue to the heavens swiftly and quickly. So we hide from each other behind a life disguised by lies and hypocrisy..."[140]

We have no idea what a huge price we are paying by hiding. For, although the lies promise to help, what they actually

---

[138]   Matthew 7:3-5
[139]   For more information on the arduous but rewarding experience of becoming part of a true community, I recommend Scott Peek's book, The Different Drum: Community Making and Peace.
[140]   John Ortberg & Laurie Pederson & Judson Poling, Groups: The Life-Giving Power of Community. (Zondervan, Grand Rapids: Michigan, 2009), 50-51.

do is disintegrate our souls, deforming them into something dark, twisted and subhuman.

John Ortberg wrote:

"God is telling us something really amazing, that in His community, there will be no more hiding, no more masks. He tells us something like, "My community will be real people, who struggle with sin and do very silly things from time to time and say nonsense here and there, but then they repent and come back to me and confess it, and get back on track and move forward and mature a little bit and then a little later they fail again, but again they come back to me as many times as they have to. They know that they don't have to pretend to be something they're not. They live in the light."[141]

The apostle James puts it this way: "Therefore confess your sins to each other and pray for each other so that you may be healed"[142]. He means that we can live in a kind of community where our humanity is not denied but transformed. A community where, by admitting our precarious condition, stepping into the light, we experience the forgiveness and healing that Jesus has generously made available to all.

Whenever there has been an authentic move of God in history, one of the things that happens is that people take confession very seriously. To the point that they willingly begin to admit to God, to themselves, and to others, the truth about their lives. As a result, instead of being left alone in their sins, with no one knowing of their longings, or their fears, or their marriages in crisis, or their traumas, shames, and darkness, they

---

141   Ibid, 51.
142   James 5:16 NIV

confess them as part of their walk in and toward the light. John writes:

> "This is the message we have heard from him and declare to you: God is light; in him there is no darkness at all. If we claim to have fellowship with him and yet walk in the darkness, we lie and do not live out the truth. But if we walk in the light, as he is in the light, we have fellowship with one another, and the blood of Jesus, his Son, purifies us from all sin. If we claim to be without sin, we deceive ourselves and the truth is not in us. If we confess our sins, he is faithful and just and will forgive us our sins and purify us from all unrighteousness. If we claim we have not sinned, we make him out to be a liar and his word is not in us"[143].

But while it is true that the divided soul desires to be one piece again, at the same time it is terrified of the light, because of its shame. Communion among us is only possible if we have been truly freed from our shame. Sadly, our current degree of polarization shows that we are far from being freed from our shame, even if we try to convince ourselves otherwise. That false communion is like a heavy burden carried down the middle of the catwalk of disguises of this age. Only the righteousness of Jesus accredited in our favor, makes it possible for us to be in the light without being crushed by shame.

So we see there is a second benefit of being in the light,

---

[143]   1 John 1:5-10 NIV

and that's authentic communion with other people. For as long as we have not dealt with our shame, we will continue to experience the need to hide from the other, alone, scared, judging them all, and always feeling like mere impostors. But when I come to the light, thanks to God's provision for the forgiveness of my sins, then I can be in front of another human being just as I am without their presence threatening me, nor mine threatening them.

Many relational problems could be because the parties to the relationship have divided souls. I think that's why Paul proceeds to make it clear that our struggle is not against flesh and blood,[144] but against principalities, against powers. He clarifies this because that's exactly how he felt. Spiritual warfare takes place in the midst of our day-to-day relationships. Like, for example, an encounter with a person who has been unfair to me. Well, instead of resorting to lies to get out of a predicament, turn to the truth and show integrity of character. That's spiritual warfare. Instead of taking some questionable shortcut or taking advantage of some tempting unfair advantage, emulate the righteousness that distinguishes the Kingdom of God. That's spiritual warfare. Instead of struggling to place yourself in a privileged position, choose to trust God. That's spiritual warfare. Instead of resorting to hurtful words to hurt the one who attacks me, practice pacifying silence or the conciliatory word that blesses. Thus, defeating evil with good.

---

[144]   Ephesians 6:12

Javier Gómez Marrero

A BRIEF GLIMPSE INTO MY UNDIVIDED SOUL

My life before Christ was marked by a series of traumas of a sexual nature. Starting with an addiction in my early teens, which took me to very dark places.

For about four to five years, I did things that I'm very ashamed to have done. I lived a double life. I was the exemplary son of my parents; and at the same time, I was someone tortured and controlled by lust and perversion. Even so I insisted on trying to be two persons. So I became convinced that what my parents thought about me was the truth, thus disassociating me from my own evil. To the point that I came to forget many of the bad things I did.

In my late teens I had a genuine encounter with God's grace and was able to find full freedom from my bondage to lust. It was actually miraculous, for I suddenly found a willpower that evidently did not come from myself and that helped me to resist. A few years later, however, I began to suffer from nightmares and to remember something of the darkness from which years ago I thought I had disengaged. Having only partial memories, somehow, I almost managed to ignore them and move on.

In my first year of marriage, the nightmares and disturbing memories increased. Then, when I started my first pastorate, they skyrocketed exponentially. The contradiction of serving God and the darkness of those teenage years was unbearable. It filled my life with anguish, even though I, supposedly, already knew God and was serving Him.

124

Just like the woman from Samaria, I didn't know who I was talking to either. Would you allow me to share more about that using the words of that beautiful story of redemption?[145]

- Give me water.

- How is it that you ask me for water when you are a Jew, and I am a Samaritan?

- If you knew God's gift and who it is that asks you for water, you would ask him, and he would give you living water.

- What do you have to draw the water from the well, is deep, are you older than Jacob?

- Go and look for your husband.

- I don't have a husband.

- You are telling the truth when you say that you do not have a husband because you have had five and the one you have now is not your husband.

- I see that you are a prophet, you say that we should worship there in Jerusalem and we say that on this mountain, where should we do it?

- Neither here nor there, but the hour is coming and has already come when true worshippers will worship in spirit and truth.

Jesus, in a sense, lets the Samaritan woman lead the conversation. She jumps to another topic and Jesus follows her. She avoids the obvious, and Jesus doesn't pressure her, saying, "Where do you think you're going? Let's get back to this." To

---

[145]   The story of the Samaritan woman and her encounter with Jesus can be found in John 4:1-30.

the contrary, He would say something like, "Do you want to talk about worship? Well, let's do it, true worship is not about external things, it is not about this mountain or that mountain, it is not about these ceremonies or that, it is about complete authenticity. True worship is about being exposed for who we really are and need. With God, it's not about our strengths but about our weaknesses and failures. With God it is always a relationship that is in spirit and truth." She runs to the issue of places of worship and Jesus shows her that in the end, it's always the same theme. She wants to stay on the surface, but Jesus wants to bring her to her core, to the truth, to her deep thirst. Thirst for security, acceptance, and meaning.

Life outside of paradise is brutally hard. But we want to convince ourselves otherwise. We go from place to place looking for ways to silence our pain and quench our thirst for meaning. Unsuccessful, we try to live on the surface of our life, alienating ourselves from the affairs of the soul and entertaining ourselves with the trivial, though without much success either.

Every time the woman spoke, it seemed that the conversation had ended.

- Why are you asking me for water? (Boom! This conversation is over, right?)
- If only you knew...
- Are you older than our father Jacob, is there a better source of water here than this? (Boom! Now it's over, isn't it?)

- I have living water.[146]

To her, that didn't make any sense. Remember, this woman had learned not to trust men. She had learned, the hard way, to handle them and defend herself against them.

Jesus says to her: "I have living water, and whoever drinks of that water will not thirst again." To which she replies: "Well, give me that water so that I never have to come here again." She doesn't seem to have believed a single word of what Jesus was saying to her. But then, Jesus says to her, loud and clear, " Go, call your husband and come back"[147].

Suddenly, it becomes too personal. That was the last topic she would have wanted to talk about. So, she evades it; dry and curt she answers: "I have no husband"[148]. Again, end of the conversation, right? However, once again Jesus is going to insist: "What you hace said is quite true. The fact is, you have had five husbands, and the man you now have is not your husband."[149]

What will she do now? The same thing we do, change the subject: "I can see that you are a prophet"[150]. In other words: "Let's not talk about me, let's talk about you; Let's talk about your obvious field of interest, theology." It is always easier to talk about the religious thing, and the philosophical thing, than about myself and my condition. A conversation of theological controversies will always be less threatening than talking

---

146   Today we have living water in the sink, but that was a desert. For them that was the best water within their reach, the luxury of kings. It was the well of the richest man of that time, Jacob.
147   John 4:16 NIV
148   John 4:17 NIV
149   John 4:18 NIV
150   John 4:19 NIV

about my life, and the shame that always besets it. But Jesus has her where He wants her.

C. S. Lewis wrote:

> "You must imagine me quite alone, in that room of the Magdalen, night after night, feeling, every time my mind turned away from work, the continual, inexorable approach of Him with whom I so decidedly desired to meet. In the end, the One whom I deeply feared fell upon me. Around the 1929 Trinity feast day I relented, admitted that God was God, and knelt down, prayed. That night I was perhaps the most elusive and reluctant convert in all England."[151]

Can you see it? Like Lewis, Jesus reveals himself to that woman, not as a concept, but as a person. Someone who knew her better than she knew herself. It is only then that he says to her: "I am the Christ, the One talking with you!"[152]. So, she runs off excitedly in a rush to tell others, "Come and see a man who told me everything I ever did! Can this be the Christ?"[153]. Something like that happened to me. And with this book, I try to do, and say, exactly the same as she did.

REMOVING THE REASON FOR MY SHAME

When you come to experience the peace of knowing yourself completely justified on the merits of Jesus, everything changes. Everything you though was gain, things like titles,

---

[151]   Roger White, Judith Wolfe, Brendan Wolfe, C. S. Lewis and His Circle: Essays and Memoirs from the Oxford C.S. Lewis Society, Oxford University Press, 2015, 6.
[152]   John 4:26 NLV
[153]   John 4:29 NLV

possessions, contacts, reputation, surnames, recognitions, aptitudes, strengths, so on and so forth, now appear like red numbers in accounting books. Instead of adding, they take away from us; for they deprive us of the supreme excellency of knowing Christ and of being found in Him.

If looking impressive, controlling the outcomes, and always being in first place, is your thing, then it could only mean that you have not yet known the peace of truly being in Christ and not in yourself. Because when you do, you can stop taking yourself so seriously. You reach the point of being able to laugh at yourself. In addition, you will be able to acknowledge and respect your limits, and for the first time you will stop feeling like an imposter. Your performance will no longer define you.

If God puts us at peace with Himself, there is nothing more to fear. You no longer need to deny, hide, or even forget your shameful past. All that shameful past actually happened; but in Jesus you are now a trophy of His Grace. A story that has been redeemed by Jesus, who has rescued it from the darkness.

Javier Gómez Marrero

Chapter 9

A Faith That Redeems Our Suffering

"God can handle your anger, your disappointment, and even your bitterness. But to turn away from Jesus is to abandon the only hope to get out of pain... And there has to be some point in your day when you let it all go. All the tragedy in the world, the anguish, the last shooting, the earthquake... the soul was never supposed to endure that. The soul was never supposed to inhabit a world like this. It's too much. Your soul is finite. You can't carry the pains of the world. Only God can do that."

— John Eldredge
Counselor, writer and
American speaker

They tell of a crowded job interview that took place in India, in which two lucky finalists were preparing to face a final round of questions. After the usual greetings they asked the first interviewee: "Can you tell us what the date of independence of India was?" "Well, that took place in 1947, but it is worth saying that there were many events and great conversations that were carrying the thing forward, which finally took place in 1947." "All right, now tell us: Who is the father of our nation?" "You know, it's really not fair to select just one person, because there were many involved, and they all had some involvement in the matter, I don't think it's fair to select just one." "Excellent, now tell us: Do you think corruption is India's main problem?" "Well, certainly our prime minister appointed a commission to study the matter, and I don't think it's right to jump to conclusions, I'd rather wait for their findings."

The other person who had applied for the job waited nervously outside, and when the one they interviewed first came out, he asked him: "Please tell me what are the questions, what are the questions?" "They made us swear that we would not share the questions." "Ok, I get that, but they didn't make you swear that you wouldn't share the answers, so give me the answers." The man listened to the answers carefully and memorized them. Waiting inside, the human resources officer noticed that the next application was incomplete, so she decided to fill it out at the beginning of the interview. "Welcome, tell us what the date of your birth is?" "Well, that took place in 1947, but it is worth saying that there were many events and great conversations that were carrying the thing forward, which finally took place in 1947." Somewhat incredulous, she immediately proceeded to ask: "Can you tell us what your father's name is?" "You know, it's really not fair to select just one person when there were a lot of people involved, and they all had some involvement in the matter, I don't think it's fair to select just one." Indignant, the human resources woman rebuked him: "Hey, are you crazy?" "Well, certainly our prime minister appointed a commission to study the matter, and I don't think it's right to jump to conclusions, I'd rather wait for their findings."[154]

---

[154]   Anonymous illustration.

If you can't give me the questions, then at least give me the answers. Obviously, the questions will always be at least as important as the answers. So, it's not surprising that the Gospel deals with both, the questions we should be wrestling with and the answers to those questions. Thus, presenting us with a clear picture of what is wrong with the world and with us, as well as what is the only remedy for our predicament.

THE LIFE OF FAITH

The Christian life is a life that is lived by faith and for faith. That's why the Bible devotes so much space to clarifying what that faith is all about, and one of them is Hebrews 11, and Hebrews 12:1-4.

According to Hebrews, the life of faith is a life that operates with certainties and realities. It is a life that resists going through a world as dangerous as this one, merely groping. Instead, it combines the true humility of admitting that I do not know or see as much as I would typically prefer to assume with the sober realization that God is infinitely worthy of my most absolute trust. According to the Bible, faith comes through hearing the word of God[155]. God speaks and acts first, thus gaining all my trust. Faith is then the most reasonable response to God's initiative and activity.

Those Christians to whom the letter of Hebrews is addressed faced such persecution that abandoning their faith began to seem attractive. The writer seeks to convince them that this would not only be disastrous, but the worst thing they

---

[155]   Romans 10:17

could do. The history of the heroes of Israel exemplifies the main postulate of Christianity: "...the righteous will live by faith"[156]. Every heroic act recorded in Hebrews chapter 11 about that story, each of them the stuff of legend, was the result of their faith. Otherwise, they would never have occupied so many "headlines".

All these great feats are evidence of the fact that the key to their lives was to do what anyone with at least a modicum of wisdom would have done in their place had they encountered such a God: believe Him! Believing, they followed God's script for their lives, deeming whatever this trustworthy God instructed them to do as worth doing.

God tells Abel all the truth he needs to know about his own sin and goes so far as to tell him the kind of sacrifice he would need to offer. Abel's greatness lies chiefly in the fact that he believes God in all that God tells him about his sin. Surely, the first thing we need to believe God is what God tells us about our sin. That is exactly what Cain did not do.

God gives Cain an unparalleled teaching about sin, but Cain does not believe it. What happened next should surprise no one: God does not accept Cain, nor his offering. Cain reacts angrily; in spite of that God tries to reason with him, saying:

> "Why are you angry? Why is your face downcast? If you do what is right, will you not be accepted? But if you do not do what is right, sin is crouching at your door; it desires to have you, but you must rule over it"[157].

---

[156]   Romans 1:17 NIV
[157]   Genesis 4:6-7 NIV

Cain does not believe God and after he is punished for ending his own brother's life, he eventually says to God, "My punishment is too great to bear"[158]. Which could be translated as, the burden of my sin is too great. Perhaps that was why Alberto Benjamin Simpson once suggested that the devil first tries to convince you that you are not a sinner or that you are not that much of a sinner. When that charade becomes unsustainable, he tries to convince you that there is no forgiveness for your sin. That is why Abel's faith continues to speak to us.

Noah's faith speaks to us as well. His story is among the big favorites. He believed God and followed God's instructions as awkward as they were. His obedience not only saved him, it also saved his family! Imagine the ridiculousness: a large ship parked upon dry land, supposedly because it was going to rain a lot.

What about Abraham? Imagine the absurdity of changing his name to, 'father of many', when he had not even been able to father one child. Incidentally, Abraham's tent life is itself a metaphor. This pilgrim of pilgrims represents that traveler who goes to a permanent place, and his whole life is a "heading towards", without necessarily arriving. Even when he manages to dwell in the promised land, Abraham continues to live in tents, because he was aiming for a city that is not of this world, not made by human hands. Since then, each of these men and women who preceded us in the life of faith, set their eyes on something that this world will never be able to offer us and have reached for something infinitely more precious that God has seen fit to give us.

---

158   Genesis 4:13 NIV

The metaphor of Abraham's tents — rather than Abraham's cities — speaks to something that the milk-and-honey-flowing lands of this world can never offer. Something Israel's heroes would learn early in the game. That is why both those who were miraculously delivered from suffering[159] and those who were not,[160] all attained a good witness through their faith.[161] Because either way, their faith glorified God.

The metaphor of Abraham's tents is followed by another that is full of meaning and that appears in the 12th chapter of Hebrews. It is a race in a coliseum. So that famous cloud of witnesses is none other than those mentioned in Hebrews 11, who now in the stands cheer the current runners, cheer us!

THE BEST FAN BASE IN THE WORLD

Eugene Peterson paraphrases Hebrews 12:1-3:

"Do you see what this means—all these pioneers who blazed the way, all these veterans cheering us on? It means we'd better get on with it. Strip down, start running—and never quit! No extra spiritual fat, no parasitic sins. Keep your eyes on Jesus, who both began and finished this race we're in. Study how He did it. Because He never lost sight of where he was headed—that exhilarating finish in and with God—He could put up with anything along the way: Cross, shame, whatever. And now He's there, in the place of honor,

---

[159]   Hebrews 11:4-35
[160]   Hebrews 11:36-38
[161]   Hebrews 11:39

right alongside God. When you find yourselves flagging in your faith, go over that story again, item by item, that long litany of hostility He plowed through. Doing so will pump adrenaline into your souls!"[162].

Understand this well, it is your turn at bat. God has a plan for your life precisely for this moment in history: a race of faith. Your life has a definite particularity, there is only one you. You are irreplaceable. You have a unique contribution to make. A career that in more ways than one is yours alone. Run your race well. God is not going to ask me one day why I wasn't A.B. Simpson or A.W. Tozer, or Antonio López; but He could very well ask me why I was not Javier Gómez Marrero.

Run your race well! That arduous race often scares us. Other times it makes us angry, other times it throws us to the ground and many other times it makes us desperate. Sometimes we like it, only to feel overwhelmed again in the face of enormous challenges; added to our obvious weaknesses. Elderly or sick parents, our own health problems, financial challenges, tasks that seem impossible, difficult neighbors, a polarized and increasingly hostile society, ministries outside our comfort zone, salaries that require great sacrifices, the mockery of those who don't know God, even the indirect suggestion that our work for God is in vain and unappreciated. And the only way you'll be able to run this race well is if you aren't carrying any spiritual fat or sinful parasites. Rather, like Jesus, do

---

[162]   The Message, Hebrews 12:1-3.

not lose sight of where the race is headed, which is that exuberant promised goal of God's eternal enjoyment.

The next time you feel alone, look again, and try to hear better all those cheers coming from such glorious stands. I do it often; feeling almost able to hear the constant words of encouragement from those that have conveyed an inheritance of faith upon us. People like Alberto Benjamín Simpson, A.W. Tozer, Carlos and Arlene Westmeier, Gilberto Candelas, Miriam Cuevas, Carmelo Terranova, Antonio and Carmen López, Ramón Díaz, Alberto Espada Matta, Miguel and Aida Gómez, and so many that God used to bless my life with his example of faith. But look also at those special people that God has placed by your side. Look to your left and to your right, to the front and the back, to all those people of God who are also running. Unlike the races of this world, those people are not your competitors, but your family. Especially seek to look and listen to the One who has promised to make His dwelling within our own being, Christ Himself! For the vigor for this hard race is supposed to be supernatural. You're in very good company. So, in Heaven's name I ask you not to run alone anymore.

It's worth repeating: "…When you find yourself wavering in your faith, go over Jesus's story again…that long litany of hostility He endured. It will infuse your soul with adrenaline![163].

The stretch already covered has been demanding and at the same time inspiring, I think that even much of it could be classified as legendary material. The stretch that remains,

---

[163]   Ibid.

although perhaps a little steeper, given the growing hostility of a cruel and perverse world, still contains many more stories of redemption to write, before finally crossing the finish line. If hell itself does not look down upon a small gospel-centered church, no matter how small it may be, let us never dare to do so.

We may have some joints, we may have many broken bones and many blows to our exhausted knees; but this race, we finish it because we finish it! Because no one runs alone here. The heroes of faith encourage us. Experiences with Jesus energize us, joys at the finish line invite us, and the Spirit lifts us up, supports us, empowers us, makes us light, and accompanies us.

THE MYSTERY OF SUFFERING

Throughout the history of Christianity, believers have visited the book of Job in search of answers to the question of suffering, and for very good reason. The vital context of the book of Job is that in it, bad things happen to a man, even though he was righteous, and precisely because he was. There was none like him in the earth, a perfect and upright man.[164] Now we are facing a mystery, aren't we? Because things are even more complicated than they seem, or than we like to assume.

As in the case of Job himself, what we have before us is one inadequate idea after another about what is really going on in the world and in our own lives. Job, near the end, will come

---

[164]   Job 1:8

to understand that what he needs most is not an answer from God, but God Himself.

Job's struggle is an echo of ours. For he at one point hesitated to bend the knee before a God who claimed to be just and all-powerful but suddenly did not seem to be acting like one. Job also needed a faith that was more than abstract theories or ideas. Because his suffering was not abstract, but real, so in his despair, he asks God for an audience. The most surprising thing is that God grants it to him. Don't you find it interesting that God chose to speak to Job from a whirlwind?[165] God responds, as it were, from a storm. Doesn't that sound like disorientation and chaos? Doesn't that scene describe our own whirlwinds?

Question after question, it would seem as if God is putting Job in his place. Many, including me until recently, argue that God was humiliating Job, that is, reminding him of his small, insignificant place in the universe. But if one takes a closer look at the 37 questions God asks Job, one can observe a trend in a certain direction that would be worth pursuing[166].

It will suffice to cite two of them:

"Do you hunt the prey for the lioness and satisfy the hunger of the lions when they crouch in their dens or lie in wait in a thicket? Who provides food for the raven when its young cry out to God and wander about for lack of food?"[167].

Do you see where God is headed with His incisive questioning? These answers—in the form of questions—from

---

[165]   Job 38:1
[166]   John Ortberg. Become New Podcast. Episode # 20
[167]   Job 38:39-41 NIV

God to Job are but a picture of how good God is. This is evidenced in His detailed way of governing, even if no one else is noticing it.

Job needs a faith that is more than just abstract theories or ideas. God gives him a breath of reality that leaves him overwhelmed, in the best sense of the word. As if to say to him: "Look at this Job, look at that Job, look over there Job, pay attention over there too, Job. Look again!" So Job finally gets to see God, even though Job was still experiencing his own suffering.

Do not then dismiss God too quickly. Beware of jumping to conclusions too early; because with God you never know, and appearances can be deceiving. The weakness of God is mightier than the strength of men, and the foolishness of God is wiser than the wisdom of men. God's timing is wiser than that anxious speed of our age. What seems to be absence is nothing but a different way of making Himself present. And what appears to be defeat is only His most glorious and resounding victory.

God on a cross. What is more hidden than that, and what is more visible than that? "For those of us who long to see God in our darkest hour, we may not always find Him in the dramatic or victorious, or the miraculous or spectacular[168]. Instead, we might find Him in the least expected place, as in a cruel injustice suffered, in a rebellious son estranged, in a temptation in the desert, in a furnace seven times overheated, in a dark pit full of lions, in a dreaded reunion with an offended

---

[168]   Margaret Manning. "God in the Pew". Accessed April 10, 2015. Https://808bo.com/2016/10/18/ravi-zacharias-ministry-god-in-the-pews/

brother, or near a campfire at night after you have denied your friend three times. Perhaps in a sealed upper room where you are asking yourself in fear: What now?

So, look again, because with God you never know. When He seems weakest, that's when He really is strongest. When He seems most absent, is perhaps when He will be most present.

Annie Johnson Flint, an orphan with rheumatoid arthritis, cancer, severe incontinence (she had to wear diapers), and eventually becoming totally blind, wrote:

> "He giveth more grace as our burdens grow greater, He sendeth more strength as our labors increase; to added afflictions He added His mercy, to multiplied trials He multiplies peace. When we have exhausted our store of endurance, when our strength has failed ere the day is half done, when we reach the end of our hoarded resources, our Father's full giving is only begun. Fear not that thy need shall exceed His provision, our God ever yearns His resources to share; lean hard on the arm everlasting, availing; the Father both thee and thy load will upbear. His love has no limits, His grace has no measure, His power no boundary known unto men; for out of His infinite riches in Jesus He giveth, and giveth, and giveth again"[169].

---

[169]   Kieran Beville, Journey with Jesus through the message of Mark. (Christian Publishing House, 2015), 177.

Part III:

AS GOOD AS IT GETS

Javier Gómez Marrero

Chapter 10

Who Would Want to Miss It?

*"The main danger of the Church today is that it is trying to put itself on
the same side as the world, instead of turning the world upside down.
Our Master expects us to achieve results, even if they bring opposition
and conflict. Anything is better than conformism, apathy, and paralysis.
God, give us an intense cry for the ancient power of the gospel and the
Holy Spirit!"*

— A.B. Simpson
Evangelist, pastor, theologian, and author
Founder of the Christian and Missionary Alliance

A beautiful story about a missionary couple, written by
an anonymous author, reads like this:

"At the conclusion of 40 years of missionary service in
Africa, Rev. Henry Morrison and his wife were finally
returning to the great city of New York. And as his ship
approached a crowded dock, Henry said to his wife,
"Look at all the people who came, my love, it seems
that they haven't forgotten about us after all." Henry
did not know it but his ship also brought President
Roosevelt, who was hunting on the African continent.
Roosevelt was greeted with loud applause, loud music,
and many journalists waiting for him to make a com-
ment. In contrast, the Morrisons left, unnoticed. They

took a taxi and continued to the small apartment provided by the mission. Over the next few weeks, Henry tried unsuccessfully to forget what had happened. One night, he says to his wife: All this is wrong. This man returns from hunting, and they organize a party for him. We give our lives in service to God, and no one seems to care. She advised him to forget what had happened. 'I know,' he answered, 'but I cannot; it's just not right.' His wife became serious and said, 'Henry, you must tell the Lord this and figure it out now. You will be useless in your ministry until you do it.' Later, in his bedroom, Henry knelt down and poured out his heart to the Lord. 'Lord, you know what happened and why it worries me. We gladly serve you faithfully without complaining. But now, I can't get this out of my head.' After praying for a while, Henry returned to his wife and his gaze was different, peace flooded his face. His wife said, 'It looks like you've figured it out, what happened?' He said, 'The Lord worked it out for me. I told him how bitter I was about the reception the president had enjoyed, and why no one greeted us when we got home. When I finished, it seemed as if the Lord put His hand on my shoulder, and simply said to me, 'But Henry, you haven't come home yet!'"[170]

I think the key to understanding the twelfth chapter of Luke, and your life, is in verse 34: "Where your treasure is, there will be also the desires of your heart".[171] The key is then in, what do you really want?

The problem is that we have been taught to desire secondary things. Things that don't deserve it. Either because we

---

[170]   Anonymous. "Christian Treasures". Accessed November 27, 2024. https://revista.tesoroscristianos.co/todavia-no-has-llegado-a-casa/ (Translated using Words-AI).
[171]   Luke 12:34 NIV

can lose them, or because they will never be enough to quench our thirst. For this reason, they do not deserve the stature of treasures. At the end of the day they are secondary things that should not be an end in themselves, and even less the magnetic north of our life.

We are referring hence to the riches of this world. The same ones that in an enigmatic parable of Jesus, a certain un-faithful administrator in disgrace would begin to see differently (precisely because of his fall). Not as an end in themselves, but as simple means to a greater good, to have somewhere to go when he becomes unemployed. If, like that administrator, you come to see the riches of this world as a means rather than an end, then once your life is over, you will be entrusted with true riches[172].

Again, they are secondary things, which while we all need them, Jesus calls them "the few."[173] Elsewhere he treats them as additions[174]. That is, what is received complementarily when acquiring the much more precious main product (such as pretzels on a plane in mid-flight). Therefore, do not worry so much about these things. Worry about one thing instead. The one for which Jesus celebrates a calm, rested and focused Mary, and not a Martha in a hurry, tired and with a lot of work,[175] which, sadly, is the one we would all have celebrated. Let us not lose sight of what Mary discovered and nothing could take away from her, not rust, not thieves, not moths. So,

---

[172]   Luke 16:1-13
[173]   Matthew 25:23
[174]   See Matthew 6:33
[175]   Luke 10:38-42 NIV

only one thing is necessary. Oh, if we could internalize the liberating richness of such a beautiful reality. Only one thing is necessary. It is precisely in this simplicity that true Christian rest lies. For since you are in Christ, thus freely having access to all that is Christ's, everything else is superfluous. He is more desirable than anything this world can ever offer us. He deserves the stature of treasure and to steal your imagination with the most avid desire. For Christ Himself is the pearl of great price[176]. The pearl for which the one who knows about pearls, will not hold back anything as long as he has it. Because He Himself is the buried treasure for which anyone with a modicum of wisdom will sell everything to buy the land that houses that treasure[177].

DESIRE AND IMAGINATION

But nothing disrupts desire more than those things to which one lends one's imagination. That is why the most beautiful lies are the main communication tool of our cunning enemy the Devil[178]. Because he seeks to captivate our imagination, and from there our desires. And if he has our desires, then he has us; even if he doesn't control all your beliefs or all your intellect. If the enemy has your desires, then he has us, since we will always seek first what we most desire.

---

[176]   Matthew 13:45
[177]   Mathew 13:44
[178]   "And the woman saw that the tree was good for food, and that it was pleasing to the eyes." Genesis 3:6

Do you want to know what things have stuck with the imagination and desires of this society? Look for what our people are looking for first. The prize that they sacrifice for. The future they visualize themselves one day achieving. The worries that always occupy their minds. The preparing they are always making. What they anticipate, look for and are fighting hard to be able to have.

That is why stories and metaphors are also the language of Jesus. Because He longs to have much more of you than your intellect, beliefs, and behavior. He wants to have your imagination, and also your desires. Because if He has your heart, then He has you.

Jon Tyson, pastor of a beautiful church in NY, a voracious student of the history of revivals, finds the variety of Christian traditions that God has visited with the great revivals of the church quite interesting. Especially since their doctrinal positions could not be more different. Including, liturgies, emphasis, backgrounds and distinctive contexts.

Once, intrigued about what the secret of revivals was, Tyson decided to take his family on vacation. But, instead of going to Disney's Magic Kingdom, he decided to take them to several of the countries where such revivals took place. He called it "A Tour of Revivals." When he returned, his wife asked him, "Did you find what the common denominator of those revivals was?" To which, Tyson replied, "Yes, it was a kind of hunger...hunger for God! God will go where He is deeply desired. God will go where they wait for Him with great zeal and with deep desire. Where He generates the most avid anticipation"[179].

Guess what? We don't know exactly when He will come. That is true of His second coming! It also applies to our waiting for His supernatural visitation to our daily lives and to our gatherings as a church. As well as His miraculous response to some of our requests. We don't know when He will come! His coming is not defined by our programs, strategies, structures, or the volume of attendance at our events. He can visit us in the humblest and least crowded worship. He could arrive at the least announced meeting and the least elaborate one.

The prophet Anna[180] knew that well. That is why she spent time in the temple, just like Simeon[181], because they both anticipated that God was about to do great things in their day and did not want to miss it. It was precisely for this reason that in the most veiled scoop, they saw God as no one supposed He could ever be seen.

God will go where He is deeply desired. That hasn't changed. We need churches that teach us to contemplate God again and that show us God again and again. Because, that's how desire works, seeing, looking at, contemplating the beautiful.

People contemplating it, anticipating it, wishing for it, waiting for it, enjoying it and looking for it first, are the ones God is going to use. Servants prepared,[182] clothed and eager to

---

[179]   Jon Tyson. 2023. God Comes where he's wanted. Accessed November 27, 2024. https://youtu.be/8W9BQAjQN8s?si=PFHGWs M9KLifThP1.

[180]   Luke 2:36-38

[181]   Luke 2:25-32

[182]   See Luke 12:35-38

see the great things that God is about to do in their days. Concerned with only one thing, Jesus. He is their treasure and reward; and boy does He know how to reward!

TWO VALUABLE MINISTRY LESSONS

In that same passage from Luke, it appears that Peter basically stops and asks (and this is typical Peter): "Is that which you are explaining, Jesus, for us leaders exclusively, or is it for everyone?" Jesus' answer highlights two valuable lessons for Christian ministry.

The first great lesson is that Christian service is a wonderful privilege. If you happen to be one of those people dedicated to ministry, let me emphasize the following at this juncture: Whenever you find yourself asking, "What could I have been thinking when I said yes to ministry?" or saying "I can't do this", or "I don't want to do this anymore". Remember these words well: God called you. God saw in you an aptitude for Christian service. The first thing He saw was that you would be faithful, that He could entrust you with the responsibility of leading His other servants and feeding them. Wow! The second thing He saw in you was, sensibleness. Proverbs 19:11 says that "A wise person does not lose his temper, and earns respect by overlooking offenses". Believe me, in ministry you're going to have to overlook a lot of offenses.

The second lesson is that Christian service, besides being a wonderful privilege, is also a terrible privilege. Jesus basically says to Peter something like, "Going back to your question, Peter, it's true, my illustration is for you. But it's not just for you. It is also for all those who follow Me. Although with

151

this only difference, unto whomsoever much is given, of him much shall be required."[183]

Understand this well, in the Lord's Church, no one should ever rush into a position of leadership. Unless you're completely sure that God called you to take it, I'd advise you very much not to take it. To many people who come to me saying they have a pastoral calling, I typically tell them that if they feel there is something else they could dedicate themselves to, they better dedicate themselves to that and not to the pastorate. I almost always allow them to look at me funny for a while and then I say, "It's not that you are unable to do something else, or study something else, it's that if God truly called you, you just can't do anything else".

But also understand this, resisting the call, preferring to play it safe, and dying of existential boredom, does not exempt you from your privileged responsibility. From the first time I read the parable of the talents[184], I noticed that it is the one who buries it for fear of doing it wrong, who actually does very badly.

The call to ministry is a wonderful privilege and it is also a terrible privilege. But still, it is always a privilege. And it's arduous, but it doesn't have to be destructively arduous. And in the case of those whom God calls us to care for pastors and churches; especially in an age when leading becomes virtually impossible, our privilege is all the more wonderful and terrible.

---

[183]   Luke 12:48
[184]   Matthew 25:14-30

THE REAL JESUS

I have a suspicion that verse 49 of the Gospel of Luke, chapter 12, must actually have been in the section where verse 48 ends. Jesus has been talking all along about treasures, desires, delegated responsibility, and the return of the master. And I think that section should close with one of the most explicit descriptions of what it is that makes Jesus' heart tick: "I have come to set the world on fire, and I wish it were already burning!"[185].

There you have the real Jesus. A passionate Jesus. A Jesus who desires deeply. There is no apathy here. There is no emotional detachment. Nor a politically correct pose. There is no softness or passivity whatsoever. Jesus is here like a laser beam, focused. He burns with passion for the dramatic meaning and unparalleled scope of his gigantic redemptive mission. Someone who visualizes Himself as a fire that is about to envelop the whole world. Someone who even when He knows that the most severe struggle awaits Him, can hardly wait to finish doing everything He sets out to do.

So I take this moment to tell you one of my secrets in ministry. Be vigilant for times when you feel discouraged, tired, or when apathy seems to have moved in with you, or cynicism, or fear of the immense responsibility on your shoulders. Be aware when the injustice with which some of those same people you are trying to help sometimes treat you is taking its toll on you. There is nothing better to get through those times than

---

[185]   Luke 12:49 NIV

spending more time knowing, contemplating, enjoying and listening to this Jesus on fire, whose presence, delicious and terrible at the same time, is better than life.

That's why the church comes together. We don't come together for practical advice or to get our regular dose of religion, let alone compete with those who attend other churches. We do it so that we can enjoy a love that is better than life. We do this so that we can drink from the water that really quenches thirst. Many of us are determined to return regularly because you never know what this living God will want to do next in, and among, us. Who would want to miss God? He desires to ignite you with a passion for Him that consumes you. He wants to make you burn, but in such a way that many more people will come to see the fire.

The question still demands an answer: What do you really want most? When you take an honest look at your desires, if you realize that your imagination has been taken away by secondary things and additions, if, being honest with yourself, you realize that your attention is fading like steam between an infinity of things, then do yourself the favor of regularly exposing yourself to the most authentic beauty. The One that deserves to be the object of all your desire, as well as your most concentrated attention. The One that when you contemplate Him will capture your imagination like nothing else is able to. The matchless beauty of the One who does know how to love to the end and in whose Kingdom, life is all that it was ever supposed to be. By God's grace, to flourish!

That is why we make disciples, because it is impossible to be appreciating and enjoying the beauty we already have in Jesus and not share it. Impossible. That is why we also long for more of Jesus. More of Jesus' direction and less of our own wisdom. More of the grace of Jesus and less of our religious sweat. More of the power of Jesus and less of our human strategies. More of Jesus' promises and less of our anxious speculation. More of the Spirit of Jesus and less of the spirit of this world. More of what Jesus is passionate about and less of the world's passions. More rest in Jesus, and less of our rush to keep producing. More collaboration among those belonging to Jesus and less competition among us. More of the real Jesus and less of the domesticated Jesus. Especially when His love for the world continues to be as intense as when He first told us:

> "...But you will receive power when the Holy Spirit co mes on you; and you will be my witnesses in Jerusalem, and in all Judea and Samaria, and to the ends of the earth"[186].

"All of Jesus for all the world"[187] it's more than the vision of the Christian and Missionary Alliance; it's the fire that burns in the heart of the Savior...and in ours.

---

[186]   Acts 1:8 NIV
[187]   This slogan illustrates the operational vision of The Christian and Missionary Alliance.

Javier Gómez Marrero

Chapter 11

The Universe That is Really There

"Let us not forget that such a truth cannot simply be learned by heart, as one learns the facts of physical science. You have to experience them, before we can really know them."

— A.W. Tozer
American pastor and renowned author

The ideas we hear repeatedly will end up penetrating the depths of our collective imagination, becoming part of our everyday jargon and street culture. We have never had the technological access to so much content at once, or to such a varied universe of ideas. Still, I think the apostle Paul could have been very well connected to this saturation of ideas because of his own experience of city life at the height of the Roman Empire.

Paul calls such systems of ideas "winds of teaching"[188], thus referring to systems of thought that manage to organize themselves until they reach the proportion of worldviews. A phenomenon that the church in its beginnings always took into account when it came to making disciples; and how much more shall we now do the same as we are in the midst of a globalized and polarized society, where many worldviews simultaneously seek to impose their favorite flavor of reality.

---

[188]   Ephesians 4:14 NIV

These worldviews whose ideas are absorbed inadvertently in many of our social interactions and customs, form an unstable mosaic of premises that looks attractive and harmless, which we call our culture. A culture which, at present, seems to have lost the capacity to promote and sustain civil discourse. Partly because of the famous bubbles created by the algorithms that govern digital media, and partly because of cultural immaturity itself. Despite competing with each other and being plagued by differences, all of them coincide in viewing human beings as their own savior. Whether through science, religion, or humanism, the possibility of one's own justification is considered as a fact. Which makes the Gospel an explanation of reality dramatically different from the rest, beginning with the Gospel affirming that we cannot produce abundant life by ourselves, we can only receive it. This affirmation places us on a totally unexpected path, due to our deceptive way of perceiving ourselves. But there's another way.

THE NARROW ROAD

Thomas Keating wrote:

"… As you move toward that center where God is waiting for us, we're necessarily going to feel like we're getting worse. That means your spiritual pilgrimage is not a story of success or professional growth. It is rather, a series of humiliations of your false-identity."[189]

---

189   Thomas Keating, The Human Condition: Contemplation and Transformation. Paulist Press, 2014, 30.

Jesus said that the way that leads to life is a narrow way that few find[190]. Something that has often been interpreted as referring to an arduous or difficult road to cross. However, I am convinced that what Jesus is referring to is a path that is counter-intuitive to us. In other words, a path that we could not have thought of, since we live obsessed with our own effort and self-preservation. An obsession that is attractive to our false way of being that is based on our own merit and self-management. Jesus refers to it as the broad path, not because it is easy and bearable, but because it is the only one that could ever have occurred to us: Justification by one's own performance. This is the difficult yoke and the heavy burden from which the Gospel of Jesus offers and can free you.

That's why Ephesians 4 is so relevant for us today. The apostle Paul writes:

> "Then we will no longer be immature like children. We won't be tossed and blown about by every wind of new teaching. We will not be influenced when people try to trick us with lies so clever they sound like the truth. Instead, we will speak the truth in love, growing in every way more and more like Christ, who is the head of his body, the church. He makes the whole body fit together perfectly. As each part does its own special work, it helps the other parts grow, so that the whole body is healthy and growing and full of love"[191].

By urging us to "speak the truth in love", Paul does not mean that it is good to tell the truth without shouting, offending, or hurting sensitivities, which by the way will always be

---

[190]   Matthew 7:13-14
[191]   Ephesians 4:14-16 NLT

good advice. Paul does not even mean that openness should be practiced gently, which it should. What he is referring to is the truth! The universe that is actually there. The truth that describes and defines the very heart of all that exists. That is, the truth received from Jesus Himself, the Gospel of the Kingdom of God. That is what we should speak. That is love!

Since that infamous creature opened its slanderous mouth[192] against the immaculate character of God, skillful lies have been swarming that seek to usurp the place of truth. Those that have historically enjoyed broad access to economic, political, and many other cultural dynamics. But, even so, the main and best defense of the truth will always be, precisely, its own coherence and its great explanatory power. In the words of Jesus: "...Wisdom proves to be right by the lives of those who follow it"[193], that is, by its fruit.

Then the Gospel has not only the stature of a creed, but of a whole way of seeing and practicing reality. Things as they really are. It is this message of "things as they are" that evangelists, apostles, prophets, pastors and teachers are called to delineate with strictly correct terms and to transmit intact to the next generation of Christians.[194] Thus, equipping them for ministry, so that the whole body of Christ may reach maturity. In the continual process of teaching and experiencing the

---

[192]   Genesis 3:4-6

[193]   Luke 7:35 NLT

[194]   ...Christ gave the following gifts to the church: the apostles, the prophets, the evangelists, and the pastors and teachers. They have the responsibility to prepare God's people to do God's work and build the church, that is, the body of Christ. That process will continue until we all reach such unity in our faith and knowledge of the Son of God that we are mature in the Lord, that is, until we come to the full and complete measure of Christ. —Ephesians 4:11-13 NLT

truth, with the corresponding humiliation of that false way of being with which you present yourself to the world, we will be able to achieve such unity in the faith and knowledge of the Son of God that we will mature in the Lord. Thus becoming more and more like Him. Leaving behind that other old way of being whose hair you combed again this morning before leaving the house.

A FAITHFUL DESCRIPTION OF REALITY

It's not just that we assent to the right teaching, which should matter a lot to us. It's that that right teaching, and especially our knowing Him, will become our way of thinking. But this will be at the expense of those many other ways of thinking, which we have been inadvertently absorbing from culture for years, from the very moment we were born. Ways of thinking that have come to distort even our own understanding of the Gospel.

Those correct beliefs comprehended in the Gospel are not only biblical affirmations that must be assented to in order to go to heaven, but they are also the faithful description of the reality that is there. Faith has never been about giving the correct answer to an admission exam, but about living in the universe that is really there, including our visceral need for the help and companionship of other human beings.

In the good, pleasing, and perfect will of God, the Gospel forms a new society in which everyone is endowed with some manifestation of God's power, for the benefit of all. Because the Kingdom of God has drawn near, and it's here right now. Both through the miraculous communion of the saints, and through God's own Spirit who already actively dwells in those who have become his, even though at times, it doesn't feel that way. Your spiritual pilgrimage is the story of a series of humiliations to your false identity. Humiliations that will opportunely hurt, because it is always a kind of death, like the death of the humble grain, shortly before germinating[195].

This is the truth: few things will cost you more, or hurt you more, than changing. Especially if it's about changing your mindset and your survival strategies, the ones you use daily amid a truly hostile world. It's like trying to break a vice or addiction. Something none of us can do alone. That is why it is important to remember that genuine transformation is also a community project. As the old saying goes, "It takes a whole village to raise a child".

I DIDN'T MAKE MYSELF

It is precisely because we all require that village that Paul uses the human body as an example: "…As each part does its own special work, it helps the other parts grow, so that the whole body is healthy and growing and full of love."[196]. Because no one can do it alone. The presumption 'I made myself' is one of the oldest, most erroneous and dangerous lies of all. We need each other. Paul adds:

> "…if one has the gift of prophecy, let him have it agreeing to the faith. Let him who has an office attend

---

[195]   John 12:24
[196]   Ephesians 4:16 NLT

to his duty. Let him who teaches take heed to his doctrine. Let him who exhorts give heed to his exhortation. If anyone gives, let him do it with sincerity. Let him who governs do it with diligence. If anyone shows mercy, let him do it with cheerfulness. Let love be without dissembling. Hate that which is evil and cleave unto that which is good. Be kind to one another, with brotherly love. Honor others before yourselves"[197].

It is therefore a radical reformulation of all human existence. Starting with what is the human being? ¿How do you come to know who you are, how much you are worth, what could become your most significant unique contribution, and which one, or which ones, are not?

The Gospel masterfully addresses our experience in this regard. It does, because, we do not know who we are! Therefore, we don't even know how or what to be. That's why we're so toughs on ourselves. That's why we are the world leaders of individualism, as if it were a virtue and not a vice. Either you belittle yourself so much that you must prove that you don't need anyone; becoming a successful person with a terribly fragile ego... or you belittle yourself so much that you don't contribute anything, becoming a failure of a person with an even more fragile ego.

In this cultural moment, few things are more urgent than to recover the sanity of the Gospel. Living as people whose notion of themselves does not depend on their perfor-

---

197   Romans 12:6-10 NLT

mance, but on having been created in the Image of God. People whose competence comes from nothing less than the living God and not from themselves. People who are incapable of underestimating anyone, starting with themselves.

What God has entrusted you with is great, but it is great because God is. So never think of underestimating your contribution. Nor do you need someone else to value it first for you to feel entitled to give what God has given you. Value it, because God gave it to you. Because it came from God, it's valuable, whether others know and appreciate it, or not.

Understanding this well is important, through Jesus, you already belong to the family of God. You are completely accepted. You're worth a lot because God created you with that worth, by making you in His own Image. You are competent, because the Spirit of God lives in you. He is your competence, and He is ready to act through you. It is for all of the above reasons that I must insist that:

> "...if one has the gift of prophecy, let him have it agreeing to the faith. Let him who has an-office attend to his duty. Let him who teaches take heed to his doctrine. Let him who exhorts give heed to his exhortation. If anyone gives, let him do it with sincerity. Let him who governs do it with diligence. If anyone shows mercy, let him do it with cheerfulness. Let love be without dissembling. Hate that which is evil and cleave unto that which is good. Be kind to one another, with brotherly love. Honor others before yourselves"[198].

---

[198]   Ibid.

FEIGNED LOVE

Feigned love is a sign of immaturity and fear. You know why? People pretend, hoping to manipulate others. Being on your own puts you in a vulnerable position that moves you to protect yourself from the other, by manipulating them.

On the other hand, love is a sign of maturity, because those who are sure of who they are are not perceived as being in a vulnerable position or easily offended. Someone who is sure of their identity will not see the other as a threat to their worth.

So, he who pretends to love has a fragile identity that is a slave to shame. Until we are truly free from that shame, our love will be but a poor grimace of all that it could become. Freedom comes from trusting in the perfect performance of Jesus forever accredited in my favor by God Himself. One cannot condemn or shame whom God has already called righteous based on the eternal merits of His glorious Son.[199] This is well seen in the words of an old hymn: "Christ alone saves us, He has blotted out our sins, His righteousness has given us, He has cleansed us with His blood"[200]. His impeccable justice has now become mine forever and ever.

Jesus makes the whole body fit together perfectly. Through the intentional multiplier effect, in which the Christian person ministers and in turn receives the ministry of others—all in the name of Jesus—we can fulfill God's glorious longing. We flourish! Whether in the arts, medicine, science,

---

199   Romans 8:33
200   Christ alone. Hymns of the Christian Life. 1967 Moody Publishers, Hymn 222.

education, sports, relationships, environmental protection, and so on. And along with all that growth, we also heal from any emotional, psychological, or spiritual trauma we suffer. Filling us with the love that characterizes God himself.

Love like that doesn't seem to be what we too often see in churches. In part, because merely assenting to certain beliefs is not enough. It is also necessary to understand, incarnate and extend the Gospel. It is in this context that the specific function of each of us is supposed to have its most transformative influence. It's not about running programs. You don't even have to be a Christian to run programs. This is a Gospel that is relevant to all our needs. We need to be corrected, exhorted, taught, reconciled, financially assisted, and bandaged from wounds that have been festering for decades. We need to be heard by people who do not proceed to condemn us, no matter how perverse the confession might be. We need to be forgiven, counseled, celebrated, and practice mutual subjection, as well as all those 52 "one another" that fill the pages of the New Testament. We need to respect our multiple limitations, ask for help, and allow ourselves to receive it, without feeling indebted.

We need a church that, instead of reflecting the culture around it, reflects the culture or public policy of the Kingdom of God. Especially when we venture out to that dangerous city that the Bible calls Babel, and then Babylon, which is where you make a living and where your current residence is located. A city living under a different "truth".

THE CREED OF MODERN MAN

Steve Turner wrote a satirical poem entitled The Creed of Modern Man, and it reads as follows:

"We believe in Marx, Freud and Darwin. We believe everything is okay, as long as you don't hurt anyone to the best of your definition of hurt and to your best definition of knowledge. We believe in sex before, during and after marriage. We believe in the therapy of sin. We believe that adultery is fun. We believe that sodomy is okay. We believe that taboos are taboo. We believe that everything is getting better despite evidence to the contrary. The evidence must be investigated and you can prove anything with evidence. We believe there is something in horoscopes, UFO's, and bent spoons. Jesus was a good man just like Buddha, Mohammad and ourselves. He was a good moral teacher, although we think basically his good morals were really bad. We believe that all religions are basically the same, at least the ones we read were. They all believe in love and goodness. They only differ on matters of creation, sin, heaven, hell, God and salvation. We believe that after death comes nothing because when you ask the dead what happens they say nothing. If death is not the end, and if the dead have lied, then it's compulsively heaven for all except perhaps Hitler, Stalin and Ghengis Khan. We believe in Masters and Johnson. What is selected is average, what's average is normal, and what's normal is good. We believe in total disarmament. We believe there are direct links between warfare and bloodshed. Americans should beat their guns into tractors and the Russians would be sure to follow. We believe that man is essentially good - it's only his behavior that lets him down. This is the fault of society; society's the fault of conditions; and conditions are the fault of society. We believe that each man must find the truth that is right for him and reality will adapt accordingly; the universe will readjust and history will alter. We believe that there is no absolute truth, except the truth that there is no absolute truth. We believe in the rejection of creeds and the flowering of individual thought. If Chance be the Father of all flesh, disaster is His rainbow in the sky. And when you hear: "State of Emergency," "Sniper Kills Ten," "Troops on Rampage," "Youths go Looting," "Bomb Blasts School," it is but the sound of man worshipping his maker"[201].

For whatever the head is, the body will be. Our creeds are not merely those statements we claim to believe, but those that our fingerprints represent with undeniable forcefulness. And only in the Kingdom of God can everything finally fall into place. Things as they really are.

Our faith must also necessarily be fingerprinted, or else it will be anything but the faith delivered once and for all to the saints. Each church must necessarily also be the body of Christ in its respective locality, or it will be just another club.

MY LIFE VERSE

Let me share with you what has become my life verse. I am in good company, because it was also one of the verses most quoted in almost all of his work, by the beloved pastor, referred to as the prophet of the twentieth century, A.W. Tozer. Moreover, in many ways, this verse has always been

---

[201]   Steve Turner, (English journalist), "Modern Thinker's Creed," his satirical poem about the modern mind.

central to Alliance theology. A verse of which the early Alliance, and especially Tozer, wrote entire books.

The words of this verse, even before it was written in the letter that immortalized it, certainly also profoundly affected the life of its own author, the apostle Paul. Many times I have imagined Paul reciting it to his own soul, as he would later help others to do the same, by putting it in writing. For like all of them, I have also often been saved from despair by reciting it on my own.

> "I have been crucified with Christ and I no longer live, but Christ lives in me. The life I now live in the body, I live by faith in the Son of God, who loved me and gave himself for me"[202].

What is God essentially asking us to do? It's certainly not what one would expect.

The first and most important thing is to die. Which, according to Galatians 2:20, refers to remembering and acknowledging that everything that defined you, for better and for worse, no longer does. For good, because you sought and defended it considering it as a gain for making you feel valuable, such as ancestry, intelligence, skills, charisma, beauty, connections, titles. For worse, because it refers to things you would have preferred never to have happened, such as guilt, trauma, shame, painful memories, and especially your many sins. In short, everything that essentially defined your identity, whether it was what you were proud of or what you were ashamed of, has already been crucified with Christ. None of that defines you anymore. To die is to remember and recognize – right here

---

[202]   Galatians 2:20b NIV

and now, and every waking moment – that none of it defines you anymore.

All of those things have been crucified with Christ. So, don't let them continue to define you. You're not that person anymore! What defines you is Christ in you. Christ Himself! His life, his peace, his joy, his patience, his justice, his righteousness, his longings, his strength, his love, and his sacrifice for all your sins. For now, He Himself lives His life in you.

Again, what is the first thing God calls us to do? Dying! And only after that, will you then be able to live. Understanding that the Son of God is the One that now defines you—"... (He) loved me and gave His life for me."[203] The only thing that really matters is that I am immensely, intensely, and deeply, loved. Someone values me in such a way that He gave His precious life for me. I have not been forgotten. I have not been discarded. I have not been left alone. I have nothing to prove. I have nothing to hide. I don't have to earn absolutely anything. I trust and receive Himself. I just follow Him. Paul writes:

> "But what things were gain to me, those I counted loss for Christ. Yea doubtless, and I count all things but loss for the excellency of the knowledge of Christ Jesus my Lord: for whom I have suffered the loss of all things, and do count them but dung, that I may win Christ, and be found in him, not having mine own righteousness, which is of the law, but that which is through the faith of Christ, the righteousness which is of God by

---

[203]   Galatians 2:20b NIV

faith: That I may know him, and the power of his resurrection, and the fellowship of his sufferings, being made conformable unto his death"[204].

Christ's blood deals with our real need. Bringing forth a way of being human that is characterized by freedom. Freedom from the unbearable burden of trying to revert by our own perishable means the awful consequences of trespassing our very humanity when we disobeyed God.

Jesus, through his priceless and unfading blood, has secured our freedom, our safety, and our soul's deepest satisfaction. Because when Jesus stood in my place, I too was crucified — my sin was judged, my shame covered, and my fear silenced. And in Him, I too was raised to a new kind of life. The striving of the old life — to earn, to repay, to prove — has become obsolete. Christ's blood paid for our redemption, buying back that that was lost to return it to its original owner. That truth shook the first century world to its core. People asked, "Can this really be? Can someone truly take another's place and bear their punishment?" It sounded too good to be true, and yet it is! Christ's finished work allows us to stop relying on ourselves, resting instead in the One who took our place. Being thus fully convinced that doing so is infinitely better than trying to feel valuable and safe by our own, either by trying harder to be good (religion) or by trying harder to be sufficient (non-religion). The Gospel's invitation to accept the loving offer of Jesus, of taking our place, is therefore the best news ever heard by human ears.

---

[204]   Philippians 3:7-10

Chapter 12

Finding What We Were Looking For

"In our churches every time we start a worship service, someone should give instructions like the ones we hear on airplanes before we leave: 'God will be here today, and we may face some turbulence. When he comes, put your seat in the upright position and fasten your seat belt, you may experience several jolts. If necessary, oxygen will be provided; Use it making sure to breathe normally and then help your neighbor. The atmosphere becomes something fine where we are going. Oh, and thank you for choosing to worship with us today.'"

— Terry Wardle
Professor, author and founder of
Healing Care Ministries

The apostle John begins his Gospel by warning that "No one has ever seen God, the only Son, who is God, and who lives in intimate communion with the Father, is the one who made him known to us."[205] Soon Jesus would give us all an unprecedented vision of God, which in more ways than one would come to open heaven wide to us. "...Very truly I tell you, you will see heaven open, and the angels of God ascending and descending on the Son of Man"[206], Jesus told Nathanael.

---

[205]   John 1:18
[206]   John 1:51 NIV

The Gospel of John preserves a good part of the record of those open heavens. Interestingly, the Jews could have sworn that they already had a correct concept of God. And I think for very good reasons. To begin with, they had Moses, they had commandments and prophets; and they also had a relationship with God that was no less than millennial.

But in Jesus, they have yet to discover that they are ignorant of even the most basic truths about God's glory. And if, even according to chapter three of the Gospel of John, teachers of Israel like Nicodemus could not understand even the earthly explanations offered by Jesus.[207] How then shall we ever hope to assimilate those of heaven?

C.S. Lewis, speaking about heaven, in a sermon which he rightly entitled The Weight of Glory, said:

> "I feel a certain embarrassment when I speak of the continuous longing in all of us to reach our distant home. I am committing almost an indecency. I try to tear open the unfathomable secret that is hidden in all of us. The mystery whose uncomfortable depth makes us want to get even, calling it nostalgia, romanticism and adolescence. The sweetness of its stinger is such that when it is essential to mention it, we become clumsy and choose to laugh at ourselves. We cannot ignore it or hide it, even if we try both. We cannot ignore it, because we desire what no earthly experience can produce. Nor can we hide it, because all our experience points to the fact that it must exist! And so, we give ourselves away in front of each other like lovers

---

207   John 3:12

who blush at the mere mention of the loved one, every time we hear the word heaven."[208]

G.K. Chesterton rightly assumed that the Gospels barely speak of Jesus' laughter because this would have been too much for us. And hence, at the end of his classic book, Orthodoxy, Chesterton writes:

"And as I close this chaotic volume, I open again the strange small book from which all Christianity came; and I am again haunted by a kind of confirmation. The tremendous figure which fills the Gospels towers in this respect, as in every other, above all the thinkers who ever thought themselves tall. His pathos was natural, almost casual. The Stoics, ancient and modern, were proud of concealing their tears. He never concealed His tears; He showed them plainly on His open face at any daily sight, such as the far sight of His native city. Yet He concealed something. Solemn supermen and imperial diplomatists are proud of restraining their anger. He never restrained His anger. He flung furniture down the front steps of the Temple, and asked men how they expected to escape the damnation of Hell. Yet He restrained something. I say it with reverence; there was in that shattering personality a thread that must be called shyness. There was something that He hid from all men when He went up a mountain to pray. There was something that He covered constantly by abrupt silence or impetuous isolation. There was some one thing that was too great for God to show us

---

[208]   From the beautiful sermon by C. S. Lewis, "The Weight of Glory" first preached at the [Oxford]University Church of St Mary the Virgin on June 8, 1941, published in theTheology43 (November 1941): 263-74, and then in 1949 by Macmillan in New York as *The Weight of Glory, and Other Addresses.*

when He walked upon our earth; and I have sometimes fancied that it was His mirth."[209]

What Chesterton and Lewis are trying to say is that the glory of heaven is like nothing we know. That is why even Handel, when he tried to explain what inspired him to write his famous hallelujah chorus from his work Messiah, could identify with that same feeling. His work, written in just twenty-two hours and which today is the one that has had the most presentations in history, emerged, according to Handel, from an experience in which he perceived the heavens open and God before an overwhelmed heavenly audience. The first time his work was heard, many said that they had liked it. "Like?" asked Handel, "Well, what a great disappointment; I hoped to achieve more than that, I hoped to make them better people than that, that is not the response that Hallelujah should have provoked in them."[210]

HUMAN BEINGS NEED THIS

Zeal, love, and reverence toward the glory of God consumed Jesus. His famously energetic reaction at the temple in

---

[209]   G.K. Chesterton, Orthodoxy. (Hendrickson Publishers, 2006), 155.

[210]   Jerry Newcombe. "The story behind Handel's Messiah". The Christian Post. December 28, 2018. Accessed November 27, 2024. https://www.christianpost.com/voices/the-story-behind-handels-messiah.html

Jerusalem[211], shows what should be the proper posture and attitude, if one can call it that, before the glory of God as well as the incomparable contrast between life on earth and life in heaven.

Human beings need this. That is precisely what our perdition is about, that we have sinned and fall short of the glory of God. In our lostness, we don't even begin to suspect how much we are missing. Unaware, we continue to suffer the distressing symptoms of living in a fallen world on a daily basis.

The darkness of our suffocating human condition is the explicit symptom of our crude exile from the glory of God. And the zeal that Jesus showed in that temple — because something precious was being trampled — says a lot about God's love for every human being and that giving us access back to the presence of God and His Glory has everything to do with that love.

Because surely no one would have been offended that day if Jesus had overturned the tables of the tax collectors when they were collecting taxes for Rome, instead of the tables that he ends up overturning. In fact, everyone would have gladly applauded him. But Jesus overturns other people's tables. Those of the religious officials who worked in the temple. I suspect Jesus did this because nothing matters more than providing access to God. The world is in urgent need of God! You and me, too. That's the Gospel, the fact that Jesus came

---

[211]   "And he made a whipping of ropes, and drove them all out of the temple, and the sheep and the oxen; and he scattered the money-changers' coins and overturned the tables; And he said to those who sold doves, "Take this away from here, and do not make my Father's house a market house." Then his disciples remembered that it is written, 'Zeal for your house consumes me.'" — John 2:15-17

to give us back full access back to God. Jesus came to return us to God.

The temple was there precisely to provide access to God—for everyone! But that was not what was happening. What was happening was that there were a lot of obstacles that were blocking that access. Men's traditions, power struggles, contempt for those who think differently, partisanship, fear of change, labels to know who is inside and who is outside. A list that we would only be beginning to touch. The more I think about it, the more sense all those tables overturned tables make to me. For if God is as Jesus says He is, then nothing matters more than having full access to God. With it come access to your true identity, access to all the help you need, access to hope, to a spiritual family, and to a love that lavishes security, meaning, and belonging.

The church does not meet every week to consume a religious product; It's not even us, properly speaking, who are gathering it. It is God who gathers His church; we are not even the main actors. He brings us together, more than to give us something, to give Himself to us; so that we can have Him again. God gathers us together to help us regain our sanity. God gathers us together to tell us how the world works and how we are supposed to function in it. He does it so that we can finally worship, as we had wished to be able to do all our lives.

David Foster Wallace wrote:

"Everyone worships. The only difference we have is what to worship. But beware, the things you typically adore will tend to eat you alive. Love money and material things and you will never feel that you have enough. Adore your body, beauty, and time and age start showing, you'll die a million deaths before you reach the end."[212]

You and I need to hear that warning, be careful what you love! If it is true that we first form our habits, and then our habits form us, then living in a materialistic society has been forming our identity and the identity of those around us. Aggressive propaganda, social media, mass media, as well as the popular wisdom embedded in every form of art that informs our senses, capture our imaginations daily with cleverly disguised lies about what the good life is and what it looks like, and what must be done to get there.

It is not surprising then that after such cultural conditioning, we go through life thinking that the world revolves around us. Including the Church, which we go to week after week, as if we were heading to the shopping center. That is, to consume a product.

DO YOU KNOW WHAT YOU'RE LOOKING FOR?

Living in this materialistic society has not done you much good. There is a question that corroborates how encompassing the presence of this vision of consumerism is in our society. You and I hear it every day, as we stand in front of every cash register: "Did you find everything you were looking

---

[212]   David Foster Wallace. "This is Water". David Foster Wallace's 2005 commencement speech to the graduating class at Kenyon College. Farnam Street Media Inc. Accessed November 27, 2024. https://fs.blog/david-foster-wallace-this-is-water/

for?" So, very naively, we say things like, "I liked the devotional, I liked the sermon, ah, and I liked Handel's Hallelujah." We expect there to be good music and preaching. And that they offer a program that is good, balanced, and that manages time well. We want good quality in the announcements, ceremonies, and in everything that is presented. Yet, in many churches we are not necessarily waiting for God to powerfully break into the meeting. I fear that partly explains the lack of transformation we are typically witnessing in our churches.

We sing and listen to sermons, but even without realizing it, starting with myself, we tend to do so as consumers and not as authentic worshipers. Changing that is going to require us to flipping some tables in our busy, distracted lives. Old habits that we need to start questioning as soon as possible. Practices that align our way of thinking with that of the dominant culture.

Many of those supposedly innocent habits include shopping at the mall, watching or attending a concert, watching or attending a sporting event, choosing from a restaurant menu, as well as from the menu of Netflix, Spotify, Amazon Prime, AppleTV, and Disney+. So, we're going to need to make decisions that could become so radical, that they will sometimes feel like overturning a huge number of tables. Decisions that little by little, will form us into the kind of people who begin to find God, something much more beautiful than any other person or experience in this world. People for whom dedicating themselves to the cause of Christ feels like the best investment of their lives. People whose cup overflows, with much more than it can ever hold.

SOLUTIONS FOR THE WRONG PROBLEMS

Our people spend their time moving heaven and earth looking for ways to fix the problems of this world. Unaware, they are unable to elucidate what the main problem is. What happens to them is similar to what happened with the three temptations in the desert, with their apparent solutions to all the wrong problems. Turn these stones into bread. Launch yourself from the pinnacle of the temple. All these kingdoms I will give you, if you worship me. Of course, bread matters, but every word that comes out of God's mouth matters more. And of course, the temple matters, but God's grace matters even more. And of course, political power matters, but your loyalty to the authentic for King matters much more.[213]

The anxiety of the human condition lies, in part, in not having those things: food, transcendence, political power. But mainly it lies in not knowing who you are, whose you are, and for whom you are. It consists in pretending to be God when we are creatures; thus, alienating us from reality. If the devil has done something extraordinarily right, it is to distract us with problems that are just the side effects of the real problem. Missing out on the Glory of God, and the universe that is there, is the real problem! Because only there, everything is as it should be. Bread, transcendence, political power? We certainly need them; but they are not what we need most. What we need most is God. People suffer, but it is because they do not have access to God, and therefore no access to their true identities, or to their natural habitat, or to a place at the table, or a good

---

[213]   Matthew 4:1-11

life, or a soul that is not divided, or to a purpose for their suffering, or to a perfect love that gives them security, meaning, and fellowship.

The stakes are enormous. So, let's tip over the tables that we have to overturn. Clearing the way to God for everyone. Starting with our own soul, which is crammed full of tables full of 'innocent' secular habits suffocating it, while it is tremendously thirsty for the glory of God. And if you're not into overturning the tables, then at least, give one of them a good slap!

Perhaps in this way we will wake up, or we will awaken someone else who needs to do so. It is the least we can do. Because many times glory escapes us even when we have it in front of us. We don't perceive it, even though God is continuously sending in our direction one expression after another of His grace. So, we live without living, without noticing all God does, without stopping to think about hundreds of wonders that we take for granted.

> "A man sat in a subway station in Washington and started playing the violin, on a cold January morning. Over the next 45 minutes, he performed six works by Bach. During the same time, it is estimated that a little more than a thousand people passed through that station, almost all of them on their way to work. Three minutes passed until someone stopped in front of the musician. A middle-aged man altered his pace for a second and noticed that there was a person playing music. A minute later the violinist received his first donation, a woman threw a dollar into the can and continued her march. A few minutes later, someone leaned against the wall to listen, but then he looked at his watch and

went on his way again. The one who paid the most attention was a three-year-old boy. His mother was pulling his arm, in a hurry, but the boy stood in front of the musician. When his mother managed to move him forward, the boy continued to turn his head to look at the artist. This was repeated with other children. All the parents, without exception, forced them to keep going. In the three-quarters of an hour that the musician played, only seven people stopped, and twenty others gave money, without interrupting their progress. The violinist raised $32. When he finished playing and there was silence, no one seemed to notice. There was no applause, no recognition. No one knew, but that violinist was Joshua Bell, one of the world's greatest musicians, playing some of the most complex works ever written, on a violin valued at $3.5 million. Two days before his performance on the subway, Bell managed to fill a theater in Boston to capacity, with tickets averaging $100. Joshua Bell's undercover performance on the subway was organized by The Washington Post as part of a social experiment on people's perception, taste and priorities. The thesis was: In a banal environment and at an inconvenient hour, will we perceive beauty? Will we stop to appreciate it? Will we recognize talent in an unexpected context?"[214].

Think about it, if we don't know how to listen to one of the greatest musicians perform some of the greatest pieces of music ever written, unless we're like children, what other glorious things are we missing?

---

[214] "A musician with a three-million-dollar Stradivarius on the subway." Diario Libre newspaper. January 20, 2009. Accessed November 27, 2024. Https://www.diariolibre.com/revista/un-músico-con-un-stradivarius-de-tres-millones-en-el-metro-HBDL185552. (Translated using Words-AI).

A PALPABLE GLORY

Two stories come to mind about how that glory is the only experience that can ever attract a world that is so painfully distracted. The first is that of a man who walked barefoot spreading the Gospel in India. Once, after a long day of many discouragements, he arrived at a certain village and tried to talk about the Gospel, but he was rejected and expelled from the place. He was so exhausted that he fell asleep under a tree at the entrance to the village. When he woke up, the whole village was gathered around him waiting to hear him speak. The village leader explained that seeing him lying there, they could notice his feet destroyed from so much walking. Seeing that, they concluded that he must be a holy man, and that they had done wrong by rejecting him. "We are sorry, and we want to hear that story for which you have been willing to suffer so much to be able to share it with us." Those beautiful, shattered feet completed the afflictions of Christ on behalf of the budding church of that remote village.[215]

The second story is that of a church in Haiti where many years ago each member was invited to contribute some money for an evangelistic effort. A church leader says that, in the envelope of a Haitian named Edmundo, they found thirteen dollars in cash, a sum that at that time would be equivalent to about four or five months of work in Haiti. Later that leader

---

[215] John Piper, Let the Nations be Glad: The Supremacy of God in Missions. Inter-Varsity Press, 2020, 92.

met Edmundo and amazed by that gesture, asked about it. Edmundo told her that he had sold his horse so that he could contribute the thirteen dollars. "But why hadn't he attended the Festival?" she asked. Edmundo then hesitated and did not want to answer. Finally, he gave in and said: "I didn't have any shirt to wear."[216] There is another way and the world urgently needs to know it. Nothing matters more than that.

Robert Jaffrey, who served as a missionary to China with The Alliance starting in 1937, did not miss his own adventure, nor did he forget the price of what had brought him there. That is why, when the Standard Oil Company went to great lengths to hire him to expand its operations in that country due to his extraordinary command of the Chinese language, Jaffrey declined. After several attempts to recruit him failed; They decided to make him an offer that others might not have refused. The letter to Jaffrey read: "Jaffrey AT ANY PRICE." To which Jaffrey replied, "Friends, your salary is too big; your work, too small."[217]

The church that works well will be irresistibly attractive. Imagine a church where the gift of hospitality is not only used to select ushers, but to be a safe place amid an inhospitable world. Imagine a church where the gift of healing is not only to pray in worship, but to put one's health at risk to care for the sick of a groaning world. A church where the gift of giving generously takes by surprise a world struck by scarcity

---

216   Ibid, 93.
217   Jessica Bryant. "Counting the Cost. Abundant Life Assembly of God". October 17, 2020. Accessed November 27, 2024. Https://www.abundantlifeag.org/post/counting-the-cost.

and selfishness, a world where few people give without expecting something in return. Imagine a church where the gift of faith continues to expect the best from God even though everyone else has failed us. A church where the gift of teaching insists on instructing a world full of inequality, few opportunities and ignorance, what the universe is really like.

Spiritual gifts represent significant aspects of life in society. These include, education, security, administration, health, leadership, economy, and so many others, if not all. So, I am convinced that by building his Church, as he promised he would, Jesus precisely created and empowered a new way of living in community. This new way of living in community is the most convincing and forceful sign of the Kingdom of God.

God himself, through his Spirit, is already making himself known and making himself felt amid, and through, the Church. Not only on Sunday morning, but twenty-four hours on Sunday and every other day of the week. Not just in the temple, but out on the streets. Precisely so that all those who are outside can witness the undeniable beauty of a way of living in community, which works well. So that when you see it, you may glorify our Father who is in heaven[218] and believe that Jesus is who He said He was.

In fact, the fruit of the Spirit is precisely for such a dark world. Love, joy, peace, patience, kindness, goodness, faithfulness, gentleness and self-control are the very opposite of what living in this world will ever produce in us. Part of the promise

---

[218]   Matthew 5:16

186

of the gospel is to make us share that same character here and now[219], when it is needed most. That is good news!

Imagine being able to have peace amid all kinds of chaos, faith amid hopelessness, patience in the midst of anxiety, joy amid sadness, meekness in the midst of violence, and goodness amid evil. Nothing is more relevant to the difficult hour that the world is going through than what God has in his heart for us.

His word to us during this hour of crisis continues to be the same, the Gospel. No wonder Paul set out not to know anything else.[220]

William Randolph, an American journalist who became famous by appealing to sensationalism, was also a great collector of art. He once commissioned a trusted employee to buy him a particular piece of art that he had come to value highly. His employee traveled the whole world looking for it. One day his employee came back with good news. The work of art had been found, but to his surprise, it had been in one of Randolph's own warehouses. Randolf had inadvertently acquired it years ago. So, all this time he had been looking for something that was already his.

Isn't it the same for many Christians, including you and me? We spend our time looking for things that, in Jesus, are already ours. For from the very moment we come to be in Jesus, everything about Jesus is ours. Jesus' perfect performance instead of yours. The heavenly reputation of Jesus, the peace of Jesus, the clear conscience of Jesus, the Father's love

---

219   2 Peter 1:3-4
220   1 Corinthians 2:2

for Jesus, the Name of Jesus, the identity of Jesus, the future of Jesus, the rest of Jesus, the inheritance of Jesus, the character of Jesus, the Spirit of Jesus, the Kingdom of Jesus, and the list goes on. That is why the choruses of yesteryear continue to move us even more than the first time we heard them. That is why we continue to be inspired with new praises. He is the most beautiful thing that has ever been seen. In Him we have everything. We are complete in Him.

Chapter 13

True Spirituality

"If you're lucky, God will lead you into a situation that you can't control or fix, or that you can't even understand. It is at that point that true spirituality begins. Until then, everything has been just preparation."

— Richard Rohr
Franciscan priest and
American author

The confused situation with no way out to which Rohr alludes, resembles what Jesus' disciples surely experienced in John 13:21-38; 14:21-31; 15:12; 16:12 and 20:1-9. They fail to understand Jesus. They can't follow Him. They can't cope with everything He would like to share with them, either. They just can't.

Jesus was saying goodbye to them, but that didn't mean they were ready to know everything, or to understand everything. For the love of Jesus sometimes prevents Him from saying all that He could say. Yet, that same love impels Him to say other things, if by doing so He succeeds in increasing our faith. That was the case with the words He shared that last night with His beloved disciples. Still, He left many other things unsaid. Why? Because they couldn't stand them yet.

Jesus is an ocean, and they're just a cup of coffee. Not to mention. Knowing more than they could stand could even

189

harm them. Although Jesus wants to share all things with them, because of His love for them, He does not. Their capacity for assimilation, which was extremely limited, weighed against just choking them with more than they could process. Which lets us see that there is much more going on, there is much more to life. God is doing far more than we tend to suppose is occurring or that we can digest. The silence of God, which drives many of us crazy and cause despair, has tremendous and very loving reasons for being so. We are just like a cup of coffee, and He is a great ocean.

Even when Jesus doesn't say everything we'd like Him to say, it is important to keep in mind that God is loving us in those disconcerting and uncomfortable silences. To top it off, Jesus adds that soon there would be some things that He would have to do alone. Things from which they would be completely alienated, both in terms of participation and of comprehension; including why He would go on without them. Jesus tells them that they didn't have to understand, but what they did need was trust. Trust in God and trust in Him.

We must therefore recognize that Jesus is enormous for us! We don't need to understand everything to have His peace. We don't need to have everything under control or square up to placate our anxiety, but we do need to trust Him. Especially in the fog of meaninglessness, and in the face of the immense uncertainty of what is to come. Even when we are not told in advance what is to come, such as those times when the sky seems to be closed, we must remember: "You believe in God, believe also in me".[221] But this is not blind trust. It is a

---

[221]   John 14:1 NIV

trust in Someone who has earned it. He has been with them for three years and has loved them with everything He has. The love with which He had loved them was totally trustworthy.

The violence they would soon experience would require a deep trust in Him: a heartless but unsuspected traitor would emerge rampant from among them, soldiers armed to the teeth would take advantage of the cloak of night to arrest Him, and an abrupt separation that moments before would have seemed inconceivable was imminent ("... you can't follow me now..."[222]). To top it all off, there is a triple negation in the making that no one would have anticipated. Hell itself was about to break loose on them like a violent avalanche. Amid such a grim reality, they are assured that God would be working through all of this. "I will not say much more to you, for the prince of this world is coming. He has no hold over me, but he comes so that the world may learn that I love the Father and do exactly what my Father has commanded me. Come now; let us leave!".[223] What Jesus would do next would be nothing but to fulfill God's perfect plan. Although that would not be how they would feel. God's will is good, pleasing and perfect, "... but it doesn't always feel that way".[224] Contrary to everything that the violent outcome of that night's events might suggest, this would be nothing other than God himself bringing salvation to our world. They had to trust Him for that.

Again, don't underestimate the fact that Jesus tells them a lot, but He also hides a lot from them. In fact, he hides Judas from them! Only John is told about it, and even so with

---

222   John 13:36 NIV
223   John 14:30-31 NIV
224   An expression I once heard from the lips of Melissa MacDonald.

signs and in code: "It is the one to whom I will give this piece of bread when I have dipped it in the dish...".[225] Even at the moment of Judas' departure, Jesus' words to him serve to deflect any possible suspicion that Judas' sudden departure might arouse in others: "What you are going to do, do it sooner".[226] And that is precisely the effect achieved by his words: "... some thought, since Judas had the purse, that Jesus was saying to him, "Buy what we need for the feast; or to give something to the poor".[227] Even John himself seemed to be misled.

Jesus acts mysteriously. They don't feel that He is speaking clearly. Why? That is the question on their lips: "Why can't we follow you now?".[228] Why so much mystery?

Jesus even had to ask for a vote of confidence "...believe also in me".[229] As if to say something like: "I have more to tell you, but now I can't tell you; not yet. But trust me. I have good reason not to tell you. The time will come to tell you more, but now is not that time. Will you be able to trust Me in the meantime? Will you be able to trust Me in the gloom of not knowing? Will you be able to trust Me even if right now you can't make sense of my words, much less my silence?"

Think about it, in a dramatic way, right under their noses, the plan conceived by God before the creation of the world is being carried out. Carried out in a way that they would have been unable to imagine it would be, at least to its full extent. According to Jesus, they should even hope that it would

---

[225]   John 13:26 NIV
[226]   John 13:27
[227]   John 13:29
[228]   John 13:37
[229]   John 14:1

soon get worse, before getting better. As much as Jesus would have liked to be able to tell them, He couldn't.

Jesus is going to overcome Satan by surrendering to Satan's forces. Forces that would soon assail Him, and to which He would offer no resistance. In a sense allowing Satan, apparently, to get his away. Jesus throws a smokescreen at His people, thus allowing the traitor to go out undisturbed, to go precisely to look for the mob that would shortly arrest Him.

We are unfair to Peter, for Peter would have gladly fulfilled his oath that night: "Why can't I follow you right now? I will lay down my life for you".[230] Peter was willing to die for Jesus, but to die fighting! It was only when Peter drew his sword and cut off someone else's ears, and then Jesus disarmed him and proceeded to surrender Himself to the forces of darkness that Peter lost it. Peter understood nothing.

How could any of them have ever understood, at that point, that Jesus would defeat Satan by allowing himself to be destroyed by Satan? What kind of God is this, and what kind of power and sovereignty are we talking about, that uses what His bitter enemy plots against Him, yet He is the victor? In the face of such a great God and in the face of a sovereignty so in control — even of the very darkness opposing Him — we have no choice but to learn to trust. Because we will never fully understand the lofty thoughts of this God, this glorious God. He is too much more than we can even begin to comprehend. Even with all we have been told, there are things that we will only be able to understand much later. Let us trust in God, let us also trust in Jesus.

---

[230]   John 13:36

Let me explain a little more about this bitter enemy of the children of God. Think about it, when Satan enters Judas, Jesus says to him, "What you are about to do, do quickly".[231] We have already said that Jesus seeks to divert all possible suspicion regarding Judas.

Will you allow me to make a parenthesis here? Jesus loves Judas, in fact, we are told that by announcing that someone would betray Him that night, Jesus is emotionally compromised. He feels it deep inside. He is not insensitive to the tragedy of someone who is about to sabotage himself. John puts it this way: "So Judas left at once, going out into the night".[232] That expression is not an accident in a book like this. The night, the darkness, the light shines in the darkness and the darkness has not been able to extinguish it.

The hour of darkness has come, and Judas enters it, and Jesus suffers it. There is suffering in love. Love suffers when it sees the loved one heading into the night. But even then, God is still sovereign. While Jesus addresses His words to Judas, He has two audiences in mind, besides Judas. The first are the disciples, misleading, as I said, all suspicion in them. The second audience is Satan. In both there is a powerful display of crude sovereignty: "What you are about to do, do quickly".[233] Can you see it? That's an order!

Satan is an unfortunate creature. There are not two thrones, there is only one, and God is sitting on it. Satan is a liar. He lies to tempt you, lies to accuse you, lies to distract you, and lies to frighten you. And he lies, especially, about himself.

---

[231]   John 13:27 NIV
[232]   John 13:30 NLT
[233]   John 13:27 NLT

He is a fraud! He wants you to think he's a god or God's counterpart, but he's not. So don't be afraid of him. He doesn't even come close to being a third-rate opponent for God. "Demons are like cockroaches and vermin, and when you turn on the light, they run to hide".[234] Again, he is a fraud. So, this promise of Jesus comes to the point: "...I will build My church; and the gates of hell shall not prevail against it".[235] The Kingdom of God is unstoppable. So, trust in God. Trust in Jesus too.

Those famous words: "And we know that all things work together for good to those who love God, to those who are the called according to his purpose"[236], are not an explanation to help you understand your difficulties, but a faithful promise to help you face your difficulties.

I TRUST IN THE LORD'S PROTECTION

Dr. Pablo Polischuk, who was my doctoral thesis advisor, wrote:

> "The Christian faith allows God to break into the sphere and give revealing guidelines as to the origin, destiny, and purpose of life within the cosmos. Inviting the transcendental into the natural allows for another point of view, another anthropology, and other ways of postulating causes and effects under the sun. It also allows the attribution of another meaning to existence".[237]

---

[234] My friend Steven Lausell shared this with me, which in turn he learned from a missionary of the Christian and Missionary Alliance.
[235] Matthew 16:18b
[236] Romans 8:28
[237] Pablo Polischuk, Depresion y su tratamiento. (Editorial Clie, 2009), 26. (Traduced with Word-AI)

The psalmist David, referring to one of the darkest moments of his life, echoes my professor's reasoning. David writes:

> "I trust in the Lord for protection. So why do you say to me, "Fly like a bird to the mountains for safety! The wicked are stringing their bows and fitting their arrows on the bowstrings. They shoot from the shadows at those whose hearts are right. The foundations of law and order have collapsed. What can the righteous do?" But the Lord is in his holy Temple; the Lord still rules from heaven. He watches everyone closely, examining every person on earth. The Lord examines both the righteous and the wicked. He hates those who love violence. He will rain down blazing coals and burning sulfur on the wicked, punishing them with scorching winds. For the righteous Lord loves justice. The virtuous will see his face."[238]

YOU AND I, WE'RE THE SALMON

Years ago, an insurance company called Unum produced a nice promotional poster, in which this immense gray bear was seen, standing right in the middle of the powerful current of a river. The bear displayed its powerful jaws open to capacity with enormous fangs in the air. He was about to catch a helpless salmon, which was totally unprepared and swimming against the current in a vigorous leap. The headline of the promotion read: You probably think you're the bear. We'd rather suggest that you're the salmon.

---

[238] Psalm 11 NLT

The Gospel is God doing for you that which you can't do for yourself. Even though there is much that you have been incited to suppose that you can do for yourself! The idea of a scenario in which you don't have the slightest chance, the one in which you are the salmon, you are not even allowed to entertain it. So, when reality forces you out of your imagination; then fear kicks in with such force that either you end up sabotaging yourself, or you try to escape, listening to thoughts ranging from "All is lost" to "Run away and save your skin".

These enemies of the real world, David warns us, are too big for us. It's no wonder they'll typically have a field day in our minds. Listen to the kind of thoughts that ran through David's mind: "David, you won't even see the arrow that's about to pierce your heart. David, reason with me, when the foundations of law and order crumble, what can the righteous do? You and I know the answer to that question David, nothing, they can't do anything".

We are not told what precipitates such thoughts in David. We only know that David is facing his utter inability, and that he ponders what would reasonably seem to be his only option, to flee! Pastor and physician Martin Lloyd Jones, in his book Spiritual Depression, says:

> "I maintain that we should talk to ourselves, rather than allowing our 'I' to talk to us... Are we aware that a large part of our unhappiness in this life is because we are listening to ourselves, instead of taking to ourselves?".[239]

---

[239] Martin Lloyd Jones, Spiritual Depression: Its Causes and Cure. (Eerdmans, 1965), 21.

What Lloyd Jones is trying to say is that, instead of allowing your frightened soul to preach to you, you should instead start preaching to your soul. David did just that. He interrupts himself, denying the anxious thoughts shaking his mind; and he begins to talk to himself.

His first word? "But." Whenever you see a "but" in Scripture, pay close attention to it. "But the Lord is in His holy temple; the Lord still rules from heaven. He watches everyone closely, examining every person on earth".[240] So, "but the Lord," is a forceful statement that provides the larger context for our faithful interpretation of events.

If it is true that the Gospel is God doing for you what you cannot do for yourself; being a Christian is also about becoming truly human, renouncing to pretend to be more than just that. David doesn't say, "I'm invincible, so throw me everything you've got at me." He just says, "I trust in the Lord's protection".[241] And this is not an attempt to cover the sky with our hands. This is in no way meant to deny the harsh reality that you and I deal with daily: Real life isn't just hard, it's brutally hard!

But instead of entertaining a concept of himself that is higher than he ought to have, David chooses instead to preach to his soul the glorious truth of his faith. He seems to be saying to himself, "How am I ever to accept the absurd idea coming from my flesh about fleeing to the mountain like a bird? It's a lie, that I must protect myself on my own. It's a lie that I have no way out. God sees me; and He still rules, and He continues

---

240   Psalm 11:4 NLT
241   Psalm 11:1 NLT

to watch over me". Understanding all things is not what will calm us down. But trusting Him, will. This certainty, "I trust in the Lord's protection," changes everything.

The world doesn't seem to be doing well these days. All the injustice, and evil, and confusion, and the afflicted human soul, make the world seem to be going down the drain; but it just seems. Because God loves justice. Because God still rules from heaven. So, I'll be fine, even if almost nothing seems right.

Think about it, typically among us there are only two types of people. First, there is those persons who, in the face of the many challenges that arise, tells themselves, one of two lies: "This is too much," and that person ends up being sabotaged by fear, or "I'm more than enough," and that person is controlled by fear. Both types are embracing compulsive behaviors that only aggravate their situation. Then there is the person who, faced with the same kind of challenges, decides instead to preach the truth to his soul, using the words that are possibly the most powerful words in the immense cosmos: "But God...!" Which of these people will you be?

In Scripture, the theme of God's dwelling place, where heaven and earth kiss, is of the greatest importance. First there is the Garden of Eden, where God walked in the evening breeze with man. Then there's the meeting tent in the desert. Then we have the temple in Jerusalem. Then there's Jesus, and in Him, God dwelt—made tabernacle—among us.

That is why the beloved Puerto Rican pastor, Rev. Dr. Roberto Amparo Rivera, wrote an entire book of Christmas theology and entitled it: "*Look who moved into the neighborhood*".[242] That's a great way of putting it. Speaking of moving, one of these days, the new Jerusalem will also descend from heaven, forever uniting both spheres of reality, heaven and earth. That marvelous day is coming, believe Him, that day is coming. In the meantime, Jesus said that He would not leave us orphans, that He would send the Spirit of Truth to be not only with us, but be in us. For those who trust in Him are constituted temples of the living God. So, if you're in Christ, Pastor Amparo Rivera would say, "Look who's moved in to live with you!".

I have news for you, every Christian carries the temple with him wherever he goes. If you are in the kitchen, bedroom, school, or in the car, you can pray right there and talk to God, because you take the temple with you wherever you go.

"But God is in His holy temple." How does that sound to you now? The place where heaven and earth kiss, since you come to Christ, is you, and it is me. And so is every gathering held in his glorious name. The real question is this, which voice will win, "Flee to the mountain like a bird" or "But God..."?

David knew that if an enemy arrow managed to reach him, it would not be because the enemy had outwitted the God who still ruled from heaven. Who could always have very good reasons for permitting such an arrow, even if David himself might not know anything about it. That incredible God, David knew very well, would also redeem any pain that such an arrow would cause.

---

[242] Roberto Amparo Rivera, Miren Quien se Mudó al Barrio (s.I.: Derek Press, 2007). (Traduction by the author.)

The antidote to fear is to identify what lie feeds it and confront that lie with the powerful truth of the perfect love God has already shown for us in Christ. But again, the question is this: Which voice will win? Your soul preaching to you, "Flee to the mountain like a bird," or you, preaching to your soul, "But God..."?

The Kingdom of God is not just a place where God's will is done. The Kingdom of God is not just about how everything would look like if God ran the show. The Kingdom of God is not only when people share God's purposes. The Kingdom of God is when God does what He wants to do. So, when we speak of the Kingdom of God, we must necessarily also speak of the miraculous. For where life in God's way takes place, wonderful impossibilities can come true. God will always rule from heaven.

I want to invite you to preach the following to your soul (you can even read it aloud): "I trust in the Lord's protection, my soul, rest in Jesus. In Him you have everything you need. Take Him as your provision. My soul, God rules from heaven. He is right here, even now, accessible. My soul, rest in Him for all that you need. My soul, you can trust Him."

Now, my dear reader, at the end of this adventure, I would also like to invite you to pray a prayer that, because it is based on the one that Jesus opportunely taught us, the Lord's Prayer, attends to that other way of being a human, which Jesus has made wonderfully accessible to all.

Javier Gómez Marrero

Chapter 14

Abba[243]

"I want my prayers, and those of my friends, to bounce off rocky mountain walls, echo in the halls of shopping malls, plumb the depths of the ocean, water arid deserts, find a foothold in fetid swamps, find poets in their search for the right word, mix their fragrance with wildflowers... and sing with the looms of the lakes."

— Eugene H. Peterson
Minister, theologian, author
and American poet

Abba, thanks to your powerful Gospel, I already know who I am. I am your beloved son, and I have immense value from being created by you, in your image and likeness. That is why you love me unconditionally. That doesn't mean that you love me in spite of me, or that your love has nothing to do with me. What that does mean is that your love does not result, nor does it depend on, any act on my part. Your love precedes all my acts, for your love brought me into existence. And that is why it has everything to do with me, because creating me was an act of premeditated love. That was precisely what you wanted to do, and you were very happy to do it. That is why I am worthy of being loved, included, celebrated and considered;

---

[243]   Term in the Aramaic language that means Father and Daddy.

and of not being the object of ridicule, pity, abuse, abandonment or contempt of any kind. All this, despite any appearance to the contrary.

My value and identity do not come from the good or bad things I have done in the past, or from what I do in the future. Nor do they come from what others have thought or may or may not think of me. So, I can lose and fail, just as I can win and succeed, without one or the other making any dent in my worth or my identity. And since the only thing that defines me is You, I no longer need to give up if I am losing, nor to be recognized if I am winning.

I am intrinsically valuable by the sole fact that You created me with that value. I am worth so much that when you lost me, you sent your Son to look for me. He paid the highest price; buying me back for Yourself and giving me back what my own sin took from me, such as distancing myself from You.

You say that you take pleasure in me with infinite joy. That's why I don't need to prove anything to anyone, not even to myself. It is mine by right of creation, and of second birth. And it's not that I'm enough on my own. The only one who is sufficient is Christ, and since I already have Him, then I have everything I need.

That's why I don't need to worry about not being or having enough. I don't need to draw attention to myself or compare myself to others. Nor am I here to judge or fix anyone. Rather, I must recognize the immense value, and profound dignity, which, in light of the Gospel, are inherent in every human being. To You, each one is an immensely valuable and lovable treasure.

The coming of sin does not change that reality, rather it corroborates it. For if sin is detestable, cruel and vile, it is so, precisely because it treats as rubbish what is precious to You. Insulting and assaulting the dignity, goodness, meaning and beauty, of what with great joy You created for Yourself. And that, in due time, to the praise of Your glorious grace, You sent Christ to redeem.

I know that it is not a question of there being dignity in the sinful condition of the fallen human being, which, although not defining him, is nevertheless his present condition. A sinful condition that I must put to death daily with the help of Your Spirit. Where there is dignity is in the human being himself, whom you seek to save, precisely, both from his current sinful condition and from its terrible consequences. Starting with returning to a right relationship with you.

For You love me, not my sinful condition, nor my false self; but to the one who still feels the need to hide from everyone and from You, my true self. Your love frees me from having to hide behind miserable fig leaves. Thank you, Abba!

You are what I have always sought in countless places and experiences. Oh, that all may come to realize all that they miss out on losing You! And thus, come to appreciate you, as the priceless treasure that you really are. There is no one like You.

Alone You satisfy me. In Your presence is fullness of joy, delights at Your right hand forever. You are the air in my lungs, the light in my eyes, the joy that makes me laugh as much as I can, the innocence that invites me to play, the truth that I am interested in investigating, the generosity that makes me feel at ease, the beauty that captures my imagination, and the perfect love that satisfies every need of my soul, tearing away my fear and filling me with infinite peace.

I surrender to you all my absurd attempts at control. You are in charge of everything, and I love that You are. I will seek your Kingdom first on every occasion, everywhere, and with whomever I meet today. I wish for all your plans to come true instead of mine. There's no better life than a life in which you run the show. Speak, Lord, for your servant listens, you have my full attention. My answer is yes, what's the question?

Abba, I want my life to always be an act of adoration and gratitude to You. Restore my soul with Your sweet presence and lead me in paths of righteousness for Your name's sake. You know everything, and you are right about everything.

You are my provider and my supply. So, I don't need to worry about anything anymore. I can take the rush out of my life and do only one thing at a time. You feed the little birds faithfully, and they do not plant or store. You clothe better than Solomon, the grass that is today, and not tomorrow. You say I'm worth more than many little birds.

Your perfect love and sacrifice expel the insecurity that drives selfishness and eagerness, and a mentality of scarcity regardless of whether one is rich or poor. In Your Kingdom life reaches its full potential, even when it comes to the smallest seed. In Your Kingdom everyone eats, even if there is only enough snack for a child. Your mindset is one of abundance; even two tunics are enough to give one away. In your kingdom one of us will pursue a thousand, and two will put ten thousand to flight. However, we look at it, life in Your Kingdom will always be a hundred times more. I will update my confession of sins right now, I choose to live in the light, with no more shame and no masks. Your grace saw me. Forgive me, for I often lose sight of You and eagerly try to do Your work.

I confess also how much I have sought the recognition of others instead of Yours, for I often forget who I am. And scared I suppose I need to draw attention to myself, wanting very much to sit in the first seats and be seen by everyone, disguised with my old ragged characters. Forgive me for judging others so many times, and for treating them as obstacles in my way. Forgive me for being a Pharisee to many, especially when all they need from me most is a "... neither do I condemn you."[244]

Abba, You don't deserve the things I do to You. I am so sorry that I offended Your holiness, hurting your heart, ignoring You, and belittling You. Specifically, I apologize for _____. I accept Your wonderful and complete forgiveness; Thank you for forgiving me.

You call me to forgive 70 times 7 because that's the way You are. Forgiveness is culture in your Kingdom. So, I choose to live and die without enemies. At this very moment I bless by faith those who in one way or another curse me, some without even being aware of the pain they cause me.

What anyone has done to me does not compare with all that You have forgiven me. So just as you forgave me, I forgive them too. I forgive the debt _____ owes to me. That debt is canceled in my books in its entirety right now. Every time I remember that wrong, I will affirm that it is already forgiven; and I will say a word of blessing upon that person(s), and upon their family.

---

[244]   John 8:11 NIV

Javier Gómez Marrero

As never before in my life, and by Your Grace alone, I am experiencing a deep and acute sense of dependence on You, my blessed and sufficient Sanctifier. You have exposed the ruin of my sinful condition by allowing me to suffer symptoms that make it impossible for me to ignore the pain. It is no longer possible to continue pretending to be able to see for myself. To make use of the wonderful freedom that comes from accessing your life and resurrecting power, I will do and say everything I do and say in the name of Christ, and not from the wretched resources of my sinful nature.

No temptation has come upon me that is not human. They all belong to one of the many possibilities of sin that the sad history of humanity knows. I must not minimize any temptation as beyond my ability to fall into it. Nor should I exaggerate any temptation as if I were the only person facing it. From every kind of temptation, I can be quite sure that I shall be delivered from falling, if I depend on Christ. I rest especially on the fact that you can always redeem suffering.

I can see that for all practical purposes I am a missionary. I participate in a culture that, strictly speaking, has ceased to be mine. Help me, then, to be a personal presence without haste whose rhythm of life invites us to be more attentive to God and to the other, dedicated to what I hear God call me to do and leaving the results to Him. I want to make a significant personal investment in the formation of others, regaining their confidence through a whole life, and showing them how we can be human again. I want to focus on the Gospel and base my identity on the person of Christ alone, crucifying my self-definition and survival strategy. I will invite unbelieving friends into my life, sharing the Gospel from my real life and not from

208

appearances, thanks to the glorious freedom of being found in Christ (and not in myself). I will try to reflect the good news, especially among those who do not think like me, by giving them a reason for my faith. With Your help, my own life will invite the question.

Craving power to receive and serve in a relevant way the enormous diversity of people within my reach. I will encourage new expressions of the church, and unconventional efforts on the part of the more traditional church, to reach as many people as possible, including those who have drifted away from the local church. Through Your powerful help, I will cultivate a Kingdom mentality that is informed by a great sense of urgency and detachment. And for that...

"... Grant us such an overwhelming knowledge of who you are, so that our trust in you is unshakable. Grant us, moreover, a thorough understanding of the signs of our times, so that we may know how to serve your purposes in our generation and thus be more, truly, your people in our world this day. To that end, O Lord, enliven us once more, and draw us nearer to You and to one another. Where there is a mistaken satisfaction with the present condition of the church, it generates in us a holy discontent. Where there is discouragement, grant us renewed hearts. Where there is despair, put hope again. For Thy Name's sake, empower us to be Thy salt and Thy light in the world, and that we may thus be Thy very force in action to advance Thy cause of redemption to the ends of the earth."[245]

---

[245]   Oz Guinness, Renaissance: The Power of The Gospel However Dark the Times. (InterVarsity Press, 2014), 30.

So now I close this adventure by raising to Your throne the main longing of my heart, fully convinced that it is also Yours — Let Your Kingdom come! Yes, let Him come!

Bibliography

1. Beville, Kieran. Journey with Jesus through the message of Mark. Christian Publishing House, 2015.

2. Burson, Scott R. and Walls, Jerry L., C. S. Lewis and Francis Schaeffer: Lessons for a New Century from the Most Influential Apologists of Our Time. InterVarsity Press, 1998.

3. Chesterton, G.K. Orthodoxy. Hendrickson Publishers, 2006.

4. Edwards, James R. The Gospel according to Mark (The Pillar New Testament Commentary). Grand Rapids: Eerdmans, 2001.

5. Eldredge, John. Resilient: Restoring Your Weary Soul in These Turbulent Times. Thomas Nelson, 2022.

6. Guinness, Os. Renaissance: The Power Of The Gospel However Dark The Times. InterVarsity Press, 2014.

7. Keating, Thomas. The Human Condition: Contemplation and Transformation, (WIT Lectures-Harvard Divinity School). Mahwah, NJ: Paulist Press, 1999.

8. Keller, Timothy. King's Cross: The Story of The World in The Life of Jesus. Dutton Press, 2011.

9. Lewis, C. S. The Weight of Glory and Other Discourses. New York: Harper One, 2001.

10. Lloyd Jones, Martin. Spiritual Depression: Its Causes and Cure. Eerdmans, 1965.

11. Ortberg, John. The Life You've Always Wanted: Spiritual Disciplines for Ordinary People. Zondervan, Grand Rapids: Michigan, 2009.

12. Ortberg, John & Pederson, Laurie & Poling, Judson. Fully Devoted: Living Each Day in Jesus' Name. Zondervan, Grand Rapids: Michigan, 2009.

13. Piper, John. Let the Nations be Glad: The Supremacy Of God In Missions. InterVarsity Press, 2020.

14. Polischuk, Pablo. La Depresión y su tratamiento. Editorial Clie, 2009.

15. Pope Benedict XVI, Jesus of Nazareth: The Infancy Narratives. Random House LLC, 2012.

16. Sales, Robert C. Planning Sabbaticals: A Guide for Congregations and their Pastors. Chalice Press, 2019.

17. Sayers, Mark. A Non-Anxious Presence: How a Changing and Complex World will Create a Remnant of Renewed Christian Leaders. Moody Publishers, 2022.

18. Scazzero, Peter. The Emotionally Healthy Leader. Zondervan, Grand Rapids: Michigan, 2015.

19. Smith, James k. Desiring The Kingdom: Worship, Worldview and Cultural Formation. Baker Academic, 2009.

20. Trueman, Carl R. The Rise and Triumph of the Modern Self: Cultural Amnesia, Expressive Individualism, and the Road to Sexual Revolution. Crossway, 2020.

21. Walton, John H., Mathews Victor H., y Chavalas Mark W., Comentario del Contexto Cultural de la Biblia. Antiguo Testamento: El Trasfondo Cultural de Cada Pasaje del Antiguo Testamento. Casa Bautista de Publicaciones, 2005.

22. White, Roger and Wolfe, Judith and Wolfe, Brendan., C. S. Lewis and His Circle: Essays and Memoirs from the Oxford C.S. Lewis Society. Oxford University Press, 2015.

There's Another Way

Javier Gómez Marrero

About the Author

This is my first book, which comes after almost 33 years of pastoral ministry (I am 56 years old). My goal with this is to underscore and celebrate the unparalleled power of the gospel to satisfy every human being's anxious search for peace.

My academic preparation includes a Bachelor's Degree in Mechanical Engineering from the RUM (UPR); a Master's Degree in Divinity from the Seminario Teológico de Puerto Rico (STDPR); and a Dmin in Pastoral Leadership from Gordon-Conwell Theological Seminary. I served 2 years as pastor of the C&MA Malpica Church, Rio Grande and for 22 years at the C&MA La Cumbre Church, San Juan, where I received my Ordination. I have been serving as Superintendent of the C&MA District in Puerto Rico for 9 years. I have been teaching spiritual formation at the STDPR since 2011. I serve on the Board of Directors of the U.S. C&MA and the STDPR.

I feel compelled by God to write about that ANOTHER WAY of living that the Gospel made possible, and that we all urgently need to reconsider amid such anxious and challenging times as these. I hope I have managed to offer you a practical and reflective perspective on this, with a certain theological rigor. And I also hope that this work can provide you with concepts and tools that will serve you well as you undertake our common experience and mission as members of the local (and global) church.

Finally, I am passionate about my family, the gospel, and the church. I enjoy playing basketball, walking, and reading. I live in Guaynabo, Puerto Rico, with my beloved wife Evelyn. I have four beloved adult sons, two daughters-in-law who are like daughters, and two beautiful grandchildren (and counting). My longing is to be able to serve in total dependence on the Holy Spirit to see a Church centered on the Gospel, filled with the love and power of the Spirit, for the glory of God, and the joy of Puerto Rico and the world.

www.ingramcontent.com/pod-product-compliance
Lightning Source LLC
Chambersburg PA
CBHW062057080426
42734CB00012B/2679